MARRIED ON THE DOWN LOW

Love, Lies, Addiction, and the Truth That Set Me Free

By

Melissa Bertrand

COPYRIGHT

This is a work of nonfiction. Certain names and identifying details have been changed to protect privacy.

DEDICATION

This book is dedicated to the woman I became after everything tried to break me. To the little girl who survived things she never deserved.

To the woman who kept going even when she wanted to give up.

And to anyone reading this who has ever felt trapped in a relationship, a past, or a version of themselves that no longer serves them.

Your story is not over. Your healing is possible.

And the greatest love you will ever find… Is the one you give yourself.

AUTHOR'S NOTE

While this story is deeply rooted in real emotions and lived experiences, it is not a direct retelling of my life or any one person's story.

Some parts of this book are inspired by moments, lessons, and challenges I have personally experienced. Other parts have been shaped through imagination, reflection, and the blending of different experiences over time. Certain characters, events, and timelines have been changed or created to protect the privacy of individuals and to allow the story to unfold in a way that captures the deeper emotional truth behind it.

Like many women, I have experienced difficult relationships, moments of betrayal, and seasons of my life that tested my strength. Those experiences helped shape the voice behind this story.

But this book is bigger than one person's journey.

It is about survival, healing, and the process of reclaiming yourself after life tries to break you. It is about recognizing unhealthy patterns, learning from painful experiences, and choosing growth instead of remaining trapped in the past.

My hope is that readers will see pieces of themselves within these pages.

If you have ever loved someone who was lost to addiction,

stayed longer than you should have in a relationship that hurt you, or had to rebuild your life after everything fell apart, then this story may feel familiar.

More than anything, this book is about transformation. About finding strength in places you didn't know existed. About learning to forgive, to heal, and to grow.

And about discovering that the most important love you will ever find… Is the love you learn to give yourself.

TABLE OF CONTENTS

PROLOGUE

The Night I Finally Saw Him

The house was quiet.

Not the kind of quiet that feels calm. The kind that makes your stomach turn.

The kind that feels like something is wrong… even before you know what it is. I was asleep.

At least, I think I was.

But my body knew before my mind did. Something wasn't right.

It felt like an alarm going off inside my chest… no sound, just pressure. I turned onto my side.

And then my eyes slowly opened.

At first, I thought I was still dreaming. Until I saw him.

Standing at the edge of the bed. Just… watching me.

Not moving.

Not saying anything.

Just staring like I wasn't even a person.

Like I was something to study. Something to control.

My heart started pounding so loud I could hear it in my ears.

The room was dark, except for a faint glow coming from the hallway. Just enough light to outline him.

But I didn't need light to know who it was. I knew that

silhouette.

I knew that presence. Andre.

My husband. The man I loved.

The man I was starting to fear.

"How long have you been standing there?" I whispered. My voice didn't even sound like mine.

He didn't answer right away. He just smiled.

Chills went up my body Because it wasn't a loving smile. It wasn't soft.

It wasn't safe.

It was the kind of smile that makes you feel like you're in danger... even if nothing has happened yet.

"You look peaceful when you sleep," he said.

Like that was normal.

Like standing over your wife in the middle of the night... watching her... was normal. I sat up slowly.

Careful. Tense.

Every part of me was on edge. This wasn't new.

Not really.

He had been disappearing. For days.

Coming home drunk. High.

Angry. Different. Unpredictable. But this...

This felt worse.

This felt like I was finally seeing something I had been trying not to see. The man I married…

Was not the man I thought he was. And deep down…

I think I had always known. I just didn't want to believe it. But what I didn't know yet… Was how deep it really went. Because before the lies… Before the secrets…

Before everything fell apart… There was another truth.

One I wasn't ready for.

My husband wasn't just changing. He wasn't just struggling.

He was living a double life.

And I was laying in bed next to a man… I never really knew.

PART I – THE GIRL WHO GREW UP TOO FAST

CHAPTER 1

The Girl Who Learned to Survive

Some girls grow up knowing what love feels like. I grew up learning what survival looks like.

My childhood home was never quiet, not with a single mother raising six kids. It was loud. Chaotic. Always something happening, always noise filling the spaces in between.

My mother always had company over, music playing, drinks being poured, voices overlapping, doors opening and closing like no one ever really settled in one place. Energy moved through every room like it belonged to everyone except me.

But even in all that noise… I never felt at peace.

There was always a heaviness in the air. The kind you feel in your body before your mind can name it. Like something was always about to happen.

And usually, it did.

My mother had a temper that lived just beneath the surface. It didn't take much to bring it out. Sometimes it was the house not being clean enough. Sometimes one of my younger siblings getting into trouble.

And sometimes… there wasn't even a reason I could point to.

Sometimes she was just angry at life. And I just happened to be the one standing in front of it.

No matter what, the anger always found its way to me, even when it had nothing to do with me.

I learned early what it meant to be the oldest. You get blamed for everything.

My younger siblings would cry, break something, get into trouble, and before I could even open my mouth to explain, I already knew what was coming.

I could feel it before it even arrived.

My mother would come storming across the room, her footsteps heavy, her presence already filling the space before she even spoke.

"Why can't you ever watch them?" she'd yell.

"Are you the oldest… or the dumbest?"

The thing is… she wasn't asking.

She had already decided it was my fault before I even had the chance to explain myself.

Her hand would already be reaching for me. And I already knew exactly where it was going, my ponytail.

That was her favorite way to grab me.

I had long, thick curly hair when I was little, reaching the middle of my back. People used to say it was pretty.

But it never felt pretty to me.

It felt like something that could be used against me at any

moment.

She would wrap her fist around my ponytail and yank me backward like I was being pulled by a leash. The motion was always sudden, sharp enough to make my scalp sting before I could even process what was happening.

In those moments, my body had no control.

And I already knew what usually followed. Sometimes it was a slap. Sometimes a shoe thrown in my direction. Sometimes whatever she could grab without thinking.

It didn't really matter what it was.

After a while, it all blended into the same kind of pain.

At some point… I stopped crying.

I learned how to go quiet inside. Numb, in a way that let me survive it.

And crying never changed anything.

If anything, it made it worse.

She would hit harder, like my tears were something that irritated her, something that needed to be shut down fast. "Shut the f*ck up," she'd scream, her voice cutting through me while her hands kept moving, like pain was just part of the conversation.

So I learned.

Not how to fight back… but how to disappear inside myself while it was happening.

How to just stand there and take it.

Years later, when people asked why I kept my hair cut into a short pixie, I would laugh it off like it meant nothing.

"I just like it," I'd say.

Easy. Casual. Like it was a style choice and not something tied to anything heavier.

My mother wasn't the only complicated relationship in my life.

I have a father.

And I look like him, really look like him. Like someone took his face and softened it into a girl version of him.

He was around… but only in pieces.

I knew who he was. I knew where he lived. I knew his life existed in full detail somewhere I was only partially allowed into.

But even knowing all of that, there was still a truth I couldn't ignore.

I could never really call him my dad.

Because he had a family.

A wife who didn't know I existed.

So every time I saw him, it felt like stepping into something I wasn't supposed to be seen in.

Like I was a secret he kept folded away.

Like I was the proof of a mistake he never fully escaped.

When I was younger, we'd meet when no one else was around. Quiet moments. Carefully timed. Controlled.

I never met his side of the family. I don't think they even knew I existed.

And as I got older, I stopped pretending it meant something more than it did.

I started to understand what our relationship really was.

It wasn't a father-daughter relationship, not the kind people picture. Not the kind you see on sitcoms where everything is clean and resolved and public.

Ours had rules.

Unspoken ones.

He could see me… but only when it fit into his life without disruption.

He could talk to me… but never where anyone might ask questions. Never where it might become real to someone else.

That was the rule.

I was allowed to exist in his life.

Just not out loud.

And when I needed money… I had to work for it.

The first time I asked him, I was barely sixteen.

I remember how nervous I felt, like I was stepping into something I didn't fully have permission to want from him.

Like he was going to say no, or maybe give me some kind of lecture.

But he didn't.

Instead, he reached into the glove compartment of his car and pulled out a small package that smelled like weed. He handed it to me like it was nothing.

"Sell this," he said casually.

"You'll make more than I could give you."

Just like that. No conversation. No guidance. No hesitation.

"One more thing," he said as I was already slipping it into my backpack.

"As long as you have a pussy, you should never be broke."

I didn't need him to explain it. I understood exactly what he meant. If I needed something… I had to go get it myself.

While other girls my age were worried about homework, boys, and weekend plans, I was learning how to move in a world most people never even see.

I learned how to read people.

Who had money. Who was dangerous. Who would try to play me. Who I needed to stay far away from.

I learned fast because I had to. What started as survival slowly turned into a hustle. Somewhere along the way, I realized that if I wanted anything in life, I was going to have to get it myself. No one was coming to save me.

No one was going to hand me opportunities.

I was a girl from the projects, a real project baby. There weren't opportunities there. At least not for people like me. So I stopped waiting.

And I built something stronger than hope. I built independence.

By the time I grew up, I had already lived more life than most people twice my age. I moved differently. Thought differently. Carried myself differently.

While everyone else was still figuring life out and enjoying being young and free, I was already surviving it.

I worked harder than everyone around me because I didn't have another option. I went to school. I held jobs. I figured out ways to make my own money.

From the outside, it looked like I had it all together. People called me a strong, independent woman. They admired my ambition, the way I moved, the way I handled things, the way I didn't seem to need anyone.

What they didn't understand was simple.

I wasn't chasing success.

I was chasing something much deeper: love.

The kind I never received growing up.

The kind that feels safe. Consistent. Real.

No matter how much I accomplished, that part of me still felt empty.

That hunger quiet, unhealed, was the part of me I never fully understood, the one that quietly led me down a path I didn't see coming.

It brought me straight into the arms of a man who refused to leave me. Andre.

And I learned something I didn't expect: the people who refuse to leave are often the ones who change your life the most.

CHAPTER 2

The Man Who Wouldn't Go Away

By the time I met Andre…

I was already a pro at keeping people at arm's length. After a few letdowns, you learn.

People tend to leave when you need them most, so I stopped expecting much from anyone.

It was just easier that way.

Work and school kept me busy anyway. During the day, I worked long hours.

And at night, I sat in classrooms full of people trying to make their lives better… just like me.

Everyone had a story.

Everyone was going through something and trying to get somewhere.

And me?

I kept my head down. Focused.

Locked in on the future I wanted for myself. Relationships weren't even on my radar.

I didn't trust them.

That's probably why he stood out. Andre.

I first noticed him one afternoon after class while I was

grabbing something quick to eat. He wasn't even my type, but he was impossible not to see.

He was tall. At least six foot five, with an athletic build that filled out his tight gym shirt in a way that made it obvious he took care of himself. Defined arms. Solid frame. Skin the shade of dark chocolate that almost glowed when the sun hit it just right.

It was clear he had just left the barber shop.

Low fade, waves laid on top, lineup sharp enough to look intentional from every angle. His cut blended cleanly into his beard, neatly shaped and glistening with beard oil. Well-groomed. Intentional. Put together without trying too hard.

And it wasn't just how he looked. It was how he carried himself.

Confident. Not loud. Not flashy. Just… present.

Like he had nowhere else to be in the world. Like nothing could shake him.

Our eyes met for a second while I was waiting for my order. He smiled.

His teeth were perfectly straight, bright, clean, all there.

I didn't smile back.

I grabbed my food and walked out like it never happened.

A few days later, I saw him again.

But this time, he walked right up to me like we'd known each other for years.

"Don't tell me you forgot about me already," he said, smiling like we were in on the same joke. I looked at him for a second, confused.

"Should I remember you?" I asked.

He laughed like I'd said something outrageous.

"Damn… that's cold."

"Well, it is kind of chilly out."

"I can warm you up."

"I'm good… don't want none of your girlfriends running up on me."

"The only girlfriend I have is you."

That made me laugh before I could stop myself.

"Is that what you tell everyone? That line is so weak."

He didn't flinch. He just stood there like rejection didn't even register, like it was part of his rhythm. And somehow, that made him harder to fully ignore.

I kept the conversation short. Didn't give him too much of me. Didn't ask too many questions either. And eventually, I walked away.

Just like I always did.

I really thought that was going to be the end of it.

It wasn't.

Andre had a way of showing up, just… there.

Sometimes he'd be outside the same restaurant, leaning like he belonged there. Other times I'd catch him near campus before my evening classes, like he already knew my schedule better than he should've.

And every time he saw me, he greeted me like we were already something familiar. Like there wasn't supposed to be any distance between us at all.

At first, it annoyed me. I'd think, Why is he always here? Why does he keep showing up?

But after a while, it stopped feeling like an intrusion.

Then it turned into something I couldn't help but notice… something almost funny.

No matter how many times I brushed him off, he never took it personally. He never disappeared. He just stayed consistent.

He wasn't trying to impress me. No smooth lines that felt rehearsed. No fake promises hanging in the air. No pressure.

He would just talk to me. About random things. About nothing in particular. About life, like it didn't need to be heavy to matter.

And that felt different.

Eventually, I stopped brushing him off so quickly. He became easy to talk to without me even realizing when that shift happened.

And if I'm being honest with myself, I hadn't had that in a long time. Not someone who could just be around me without wanting something in return.

Over time, those quick conversations turned into longer ones.

We'd sit in the parking lot for hours, just talking until time started to feel less important. Sometimes we'd grab food after my classes. Nothing forced. Nothing defined. Just time shared.

And little by little, he became part of my routine, like he'd always existed in it. Like he'd found spaces in my life I didn't even realize were empty.

He made me laugh more than I expected to.

And he listened, really listened, when I talked about school… about work… about the life I was trying to build for myself.

And when I started talking about my dreams, he didn't shut me down.

He encouraged me.

That's when things started to shift between us.

For the first time in a long time, I felt seen, not for what I could do, not for how strong I had learned to be, but just… me.

One night, after yet another conversation that stretched well past midnight, Andre looked at me with a seriousness that made the air between us feel different.

"You know," he said, leaning back in his seat like he had been holding that thought for a while, "you don't let people get close to you."

I lifted an eyebrow and turned fully toward him, studying his face.

"And how long did it take you to figure that out?" I asked.

He shrugged, like it wasn't something he needed credit for.

"Long enough."

I looked away before he could read too much into my face, turning my gaze toward the window instead. The glass reflected a version of me I didn't always recognize.

The truth was…

He wasn't wrong.

And I didn't like that he could see it so clearly.

There was a pause before he spoke again.

"Good thing I'm patient," he said.

A small laugh slipped out of me before I could stop it, more disbelief than humor. I shook my head slightly.

"You're wasting your time," I said.

And I meant it.

But he only smiled, calm and unbothered.

"Maybe."

It wasn't the word. It was the way he said it steady, certain.

Like he had already decided something I hadn't agreed to yet.

Like leaving was never part of his plan.

And strangely… that idea didn't feel comforting.

It felt dangerous.

Andre noticed early that I wasn't like most women he'd met. I didn't care for parties, or noise, or being seen in places just for the sake of it.

I wasn't interested in gossip or surface-level conversations. Small talk drained me.

Most of my conversations lived elsewhere, work, school, the future I was trying so hard to build with my own hands.

One night, we were standing outside my car, talking like we always did, when he asked the question everybody eventually asks.

"So, what exactly do you do again?" he said.

I leaned back against the door and crossed my arms, letting the night air settle around me.

"I'm an RN," I said. "But not the hospital kind… I'm in cosmetic nursing."

He smiled, waiting like there was more.

"I'm also a cosmetologist with an advanced esthetician license," I added.

He raised a brow slightly, like he was trying to connect all the pieces. "That's a lot."

I let out a small laugh. "Yeah… basically I do medical skincare. Microneedling, laser hair removal, facials, Botox, fillers… that kind of thing."

"And sometimes hair on the side when I feel like it," I added.

He nodded slowly, still watching me. "So basically… you make ugly people look good."

I smirked. "Something like that. But my clients are already good-looking… I just enhance what's there." I paused, then tilted my head. "Maybe I can hook you up with one of them."

He laughed, shaking his head. "I've already got a woman… you."

Heat rushed to my face before I could stop it, but I covered it with a look. "Okay…"

Then I leaned in slightly, shifting the subject back to me. "So why school?"

"Because I want more. That's not my end goal," I said.

He tilted his head. "What's the end goal?"

I hesitated for a second, my gaze drifting past him into the distance. Small talk wasn't what this was for me. This wasn't casual. This was everything.

"I'm in school for my master's," I said, slower now, more grounded. "So I can become a nurse practitioner."

He let out a low whistle. "Damn… you're not playing around."

I shook my head once. "I'm not."

My voice dropped a little, but it held more weight than before.

"I want my own medical spa one day."

Not just a suite. Not something small or temporary.

"My own building. My own team." I paused, feeling it settle deeper in my chest as I said it out loud. "And eventually… a franchise."

The vision wasn't abstract. It was already forming in my mind like something I could almost reach.

"I want people working with me," I added, "building something real."

He didn't respond right away.

He just stood there, watching me.

Really watching me.

It didn't feel like he was just hearing me anymore, it felt like he was studying me, like I was something he was trying to understand without interrupting.

"You different," he finally said.

I gave a small smirk. "I know."

But it wasn't simple confidence. It was something I had learned to wear.

Because being "different" had never made life easier.

It meant I had to move smarter. Think faster. Stay guarded.

He was still looking at me like I wasn't easy to read.

And for some reason… he seemed to like that.

I didn't add anything else.

I didn't need to.

Because I had spent my whole life being different.

Not by choice.

But by survival.

CHAPTER 3

I never planned for Andre to become part of my life. But somehow…

that's exactly what happened.

Without either of us ever really saying it out loud.

What started as quick conversations outside restaurants and classrooms slowly turned into a routine.

Something steady. Familiar.

He started showing up more often, like it made sense for him to be there.

Sometimes he'd meet me after class just to walk me to my car.

Other times, he'd call me out of nowhere.

"Did you eat yet?"

"No… not yet."

"Girl, you work too much," he said one night.

I rolled my eyes. "Somebody has to."

He laughed, soft and easy. "You always act like you're carrying the whole world on your shoulders."

I didn't respond.

Because I was.

Depending on people never felt safe for me.

I learned early that the only person I could truly count on was myself.

And somehow… he seemed to understand that.

Without me explaining it. Without me having to open up parts of myself I wasn't ready to touch.

And maybe that was why I started letting him stay around a little longer.

One evening after class, I did something I normally wouldn't.

I invited him over.

It wasn't anything serious. Just pizza. Conversation. Nothing more.

When he walked into my place, his eyes moved around the room slowly, like he was trying to understand me through it.

"Excuse the mess," I said, suddenly aware of everything I usually ignored.

"You live by yourself?" he asked.

"Yeah."

"Nice place."

I shrugged, like it didn't matter as much as it actually did.

I wanted something bigger, something better. But this worked for now.

A small condo in downtown Los Angeles… right between school and work.

It was simple. But it was mine.

Floor-to-ceiling windows stretched across the living room, flooding the space with light so bright I barely needed lamps during the day. On clear days, the Hollywood Sign sat faintly in the distance, like a quiet reminder that I was here, really here.

The space leaned into soft tones, beige, tan, hints of blush pink. Little choices that made it feel warm… feminine… intentional. Put together in a way that felt like me, even if I'd had to build it piece by piece.

A canopy bed sat in the corner of the bedroom, draped in light fabric that shifted whenever the windows were open, like it was breathing with the room. Plants lived in different corners, as if they had slowly claimed their own space without asking permission.

Ostrich feathers stood in a tall vase by the window. Small details, but they grounded the place. Made it feel lived in. Made it feel like mine.

Books were everywhere, on the kitchen counter, scattered across the living room table. Some open, some stacked like they'd been left mid-thought. It wasn't perfect. Nothing about it was.

But it was the first thing I had ever truly owned… outside of my car.

"I work hard for it," I said.

He nodded, but his eyes didn't settle. They kept moving, over the windows, the furniture, the books, before coming back to me like he was trying to place everything into a mental frame.

"You did all this by yourself?" he asked, curiosity threading through his tone.

"Yeah," I nodded.

A small smile pulled at his mouth, but it didn't fully reach his eyes. "Okay… I see you," he said.

That night, we stayed on the couch for hours, just talking. About childhood. About dreams. About the kind of life we both wanted but didn't always know how to name.

He made me laugh harder than I expected to like something in me loosened without permission.

And somewhere in the middle of all of it, I felt something close to comfort. Not loud. Not dramatic. Just… steady.

As the night got later, he stretched and glanced around the room. "You kicking me out or what?" he joked.

I smirked. "Probably."

But neither of us moved.

I could tell he didn't want to leave. And I didn't ask him to.

The room seemed to quiet in a way that didn't feel natural, like even the air had slowed down just to stretch that moment out between us.

He shifted a little closer, small, almost hesitant, but enough for me to feel it. That space between us changed without either of us saying a word.

My heart picked up, just slightly, like it had noticed something before my mind did. I could feel his presence more clearly now. Warm. Steady. Real.

His eyes stayed on me a second longer than before, like he was trying to read something I hadn't learned how to say out loud yet. And I didn't look away.

Something about that moment didn't feel like it needed to be rushed, explained, or interrupted. It just… existed.

And I didn't realize it then.

But the people who enter your life without pressure, without forcing their way in or trying too hard to be seen, are usually the ones who end up changing everything.

PART II – SEARCHING FOR LOVE

CHAPTER 4

The Night That Changed Everything

I've always been careful about the lines I draw with people. Friendship felt safe, clean, uncomplicated. No expectations. No heartbreak waiting at the end of it.

And that's exactly what he was supposed to be. Just a friend.

But the most complicated relationships don't announce themselves. They start in the simplest ways.

It was a Friday night when everything shifted.

I had just finished a week that felt like it had no end, clinicals, studying, checking in on my clients… I was running on fumes. Exhausted in a way that sat deep in my bones. Physically. Mentally. Everything.

My phone rang.

It was him.

"Hey love… you busy?" he asked.

I let out a small breath, leaning back for a second before answering. "Always."

"Take a break," he said. "I'm taking you out."

I laughed softly, already picturing my responsibilities piling up in my head. "You trying to get me in trouble with my responsibilities?"

"Nah," he said, easy and sure. "I'm trying to remind you that you're human."

And somehow…

He convinced me.

Later that night, we were at my place.

A bottle of reposado tequila sat on the table, half-forgotten between us. Anita Baker played low in the background, her voice filling the quiet spaces like something familiar trying to soften the edges of the day.

For the first time all week, the atmosphere felt lighter.

Like the world outside had stopped asking so much of me.

He poured another drink while I kicked off my shoes and sank deeper into the couch, letting my body finally exhale.

"You know," he said, handing me the glass, "you always look like you're carrying the whole world on your shoulders."

I took it, fingers wrapping around the cool glass.

"That's because I am," I said simply.

He shook his head like he didn't agree, like he refused to accept it. "You don't have to be strong all the time."

A quiet laugh slipped out of me, not because it was funny, but because I didn't know what else to do with that kind of statement. I'd started to imagine a softer life… one where I wasn't always holding everything together.

"Who else is going to be strong for me?" I asked.

"Me," he said, without hesitation.

The conversation drifted after that… like it always did.

From childhood. To dreams. To goals. To everything sitting in between the lines of who we were becoming.

"You really got it mapped out," he said at one point.

I nodded, no hesitation at all.

"Yeah," I said. "I didn't survive everything I've been through just to live a basic life."

A pause.

Then, half-laughing, half-challenging the air between us, I added,

"Do I look like a basic bitch?"

He looked at me for a moment, like he was trying to read something I hadn't even said out loud.

"You different," he said finally.

I smirked, leaning back slightly. "I know."

The tequila was starting to settle now, softening the edges of everything. The music kept playing in the background, low and steady, like it didn't care what was happening between us.

And somewhere along the way, time stopped feeling important.

At some point, I noticed the space between us had changed. The couch no longer felt wide. Our knees were touching now, lightly, almost accidentally, but not really.

I felt it then. That quiet shift in the air. The kind you don't name because once you do, it becomes real.

His expression softened when he looked at me again.

"You know I liked you the first time I saw you," he said.

I let out a small smile, trying to keep things light. "You're persistent. I'll give you that."

"I'm serious," he added, his voice steadier this time.

And something about the way he said it made everything feel still for a second. Like the room itself had paused to listen.

Before I could overthink it, before I could step back into logic or caution, he leaned in.

And kissed me.

For a split second, I did think about pulling away.

But I didn't.

The moment stayed. It didn't rush. It deepened instead, like it had been waiting for permission to exist.

Somewhere between the music still humming in the room and the warmth of the alcohol in my system, the line I had been so careful about holding onto… disappeared.

That night, we kissed like nothing else existed outside of that space.

His hands moved with a gentleness that surprised me, tracing, holding, grounding me all at once. He touched me like he wasn't in a hurry to get anywhere, like time didn't matter either.

And I remember thinking how soft his hands were. Not rough, not rushed… just careful. Like he'd never spent his life breaking them against hard work or hardship.

I felt myself slipping into something lighter, something unreal. Like I was floating, untethered, suspended in a moment I didn't fully understand but didn't want to leave either.

We crossed a boundary I hadn't planned to cross.

And by the time morning came, nothing between us would feel the same again.

But in that moment, none of that existed yet.

I believed quietly, desperately, that maybe… just maybe… I had finally found someone worth staying for.

Or maybe I had just convinced myself I had.

CHAPTER 5

"You're Mine Now"

Morning light crept through the blinds, stretching across my bedroom floor. For a moment, I forgot he was there.

Then I rolled over, and saw him lying beside me.

Just like that, everything from the night before came rushing back.

I stared at the ceiling, trying to figure out what I was supposed to say first.

He stirred slowly, stretching his arms before turning his head toward me. A slow smile spread across his face.

"Well… good morning."

I let out a nervous laugh. "Don't be weird."

He sat up, running his hands over his face before looking back at me. "It's not weird," he said.

"It kind of is," I muttered.

He shook his head. "No… it's not." Then, after a pause, like it was the most natural thing in the world, he added, "You're mine now."

I blinked.

"Excuse me?"

He grinned like he hadn't just shifted the air in the room. Like it made perfect sense.

"I'm serious."

I shook my head, letting out a short laugh to brush it off. "You're crazy."

"Maybe," he said. "But I meant what I said."

I exhaled, dismissing it like it was nothing. "We'll see."

I tried to play it off like confidence… like jokes… like whatever. But the way he said it didn't sit right with me. It lingered in a way I didn't have words for.

I got up to start my day. He didn't move.

I glanced over at him still lounging there like he paid rent.

"Don't you have somewhere to be?" I asked, raising an eyebrow.

"Nah… not today. I'm chilling," he said, way too relaxed.

I smirked, grabbing my things. "Mmm… must be nice. Well, I actually have a life, so I'm gonna need you to get your stuff and hit the road, Jack."

He laughed, sitting up. "Oh, so you putting me out now?"

I walked past him, brushing against him just enough to make my point. "No… I'm kicking you out. Don't get it twisted."

He grinned. "You cold."

"Please," I shot back, glancing over my shoulder. "You'll be back."

He stood slowly, still smiling like he knew something I didn't.

Grabbed his jacket… then pulled me in just enough to press a kiss to my forehead.

"Call me when you get settled at work," he said. I didn't.

The next time he came over, he brought a toothbrush.

"Just in case," he said, like it meant nothing.

At first, it was little things.

Things you don't really question.

A hoodie draped over the back of my chair a few days later. Sneakers by the door after that. Then a gym bag.

Each time I noticed something new, he brushed it off.

"I'll grab it later," he would say.

But later never came.

Weeks passed like that.

He stopped visiting and started staying.

Some days he was there more than he wasn't, cooking when I got home, leaning over my notes while I studied, correcting me softly when I got stuck.

Moving through my space like it already belonged to him.

And slowly, without me fully naming it, he started to feel like part of my home. Like he had always been there.

One night, I was finishing a paper for school when I looked up and saw him in the kitchen.

Opening cabinets. Pouring juice.

Completely at ease.

"Wait a minute," I said.

He turned, calm. "What?"

"Do you live here now?"

He laughed, like I had said something obvious.

"I mean… I stay here a lot."

"That's not the same thing."

He walked over and kissed my forehead, unbothered.

"You like having me here."

I rolled my eyes, but I didn't argue. Because it was true.

He made things easier.

He helped around the house. Cooked sometimes. Picked up groceries without asking.

And if I was honest…

I liked coming home to someone. I liked not feeling alone in the quiet. I liked the idea that someone chose to stay.

So I didn't push it.

He wasn't just staying over anymore.

He was moving in.

Quietly.

Piece by piece.

Without permission.

And once he made himself comfortable in my life, it felt like he had no intention of ever leaving.

CHAPTER 6

The Illusion of Stability

Life with Andre felt almost perfect. Things moved fast, too fast, if I'm being honest with myself.

And still, every now and then, there was that small voice in the back of my mind, quiet but persistent, telling me to slow down. I ignored it every time.

For the first time in a long time, I felt like I had someone solid in my corner. He had slipped into my life so naturally that I barely noticed where I ended and where he began.

I'd come home from long days, work, school, clinicals, and he'd already be there. Stretched out on the couch like he belonged there, TV humming in the background. Sometimes dinner was already done. Other times, he'd just glance up, smile like it was the most normal thing in the world, and ask about my day.

It felt… real. Domestic in a way I hadn't known I was craving. Like I was finally living that soft life people talk about.

And slowly, without any dramatic moment I could point to, he stopped leaving.

The gym bag by the door became clothes folded into my closet.

His toothbrush turned into a full row of products in my

bathroom.

The empty drawer in my dresser… eventually wasn't empty anymore.

It was his.

And I noticed it.

But I didn't question it. I let it happen.

I told myself this was what relationships were supposed to look like, two people building something together, step by step, without overthinking it.

One evening, I was at the kitchen table, laptop open, buried in schoolwork and studying when he walked in from the living room. He leaned against the counter like he had nowhere else to be.

"You always studying," he said.

"That's how degrees work," I replied without looking up.

He laughed softly. "You're going to be rich one day."

"That's the plan."

I paused for a second, my eyes still on the screen.

"I'll be happy when I'm living it."

He stepped a little closer.

"You already doing everything now, right? … why continue with school?"

"Mhm."

That made me look up at him.

"Because this degree sets me apart from everyone else," I said.

Then I added, quieter but firm, "Remember you said it... I'm different."

He nodded slowly.

"Well... when you become rich, don't forget about the little people," I said with a smirk.

We always ended up on me, my goals, my plans. I tilted my head at him. "What about you, Andre? What do you want... how do you see your life?"

He leaned back like he had it all figured out.

"I've got goals. I'm ambitious... just not like you. But I do want to get into contracting... maybe real estate investing too."

I raised an eyebrow, a slow smile pulling at my face. "Oh, so you've got plans..."

"Yeah," he said, nodding.

I stepped a little closer, folding my arms. "So how are we making this happen?"

He hesitated. Just for a second, but I caught it.

"It's timing," he said finally. "I just need to get everything lined up."

"Mmm," I hummed, tilting my head. "Don't let time pass you by..."

My eyes stayed on him a moment longer than necessary.

"You know you could get everything lined up now," I added softly. "You just have to make the first move. Like you did with me… you were persistent."

He smiled, but it didn't fully reach his eyes this time.

I laughed anyway.

It came out light, playful, but it wasn't a joke. I was serious.

He needed to do more with his life if he was going to continue being with me.

Don't get me wrong, he had a job.

He helped with groceries. Paid small bills here and there. He showed up… and it showed me he was responsible.

He felt like everything I needed in some ways.

He celebrated my wins like they were his own.

Looked at me with this quiet pride that made me feel seen in a way I hadn't felt before.

But even in those good moments, there were things I couldn't quite explain.

Sometimes he would disappear for hours. No calls. No texts.

And when he came back, it was always the same answer.

"With the boys."

At first, it didn't seem like a big deal. I told myself that.

Everybody has friends.

Everybody needs space.

I had more things to focus on that kept me busy.

But the more I paid attention… the more I noticed.

When he'd come back smelling like alcohol, I tried not to

think too much of it. I asked once, keeping my tone light.

"Going out with your boys again?"

He shrugged like it was nothing. "Yeah… be back later."

And I let it go. I trusted him. Or at least… I tried to.

I didn't have time to babysit a grown man. Still…

Something about it didn't sit right with me. It lingered quiet, uncomfortable, like a thought I couldn't fully shake off.

But I pushed it down anyway.

I told myself I just needed to heal from my past.

Learn how to trust. Stop overthinking. Let him be where he said he was.

I had spent my whole life learning how to ignore what didn't feel right. Learning how to silence that voice inside me.

To choose peace… even when it wasn't real.

It was easier that way.

Easier than asking questions I wasn't ready to hear the answers to. Easier than facing the possibility that something wasn't just off… something was wrong.

So I kept moving. Focused on work. Focused on school. Focused on the life I was building for myself.

While the truth was moving quietly behind my back.

While I was building a future… he was building something too.

Secrets.

And those secrets…

would eventually destroy everything I thought we had.

PART III – THE ILLUSION OF A PERFECT LIFE

CHAPTER 7

The Proposal

Just a year before…

Andre was just the persistent guy who wouldn't leave me alone, the one I kept friend-zoning.

He wasn't like the typical guys I go for, don't get me wrong. He was handsome, yeah… but he was cocky. Not hood. More suburban.

We came from completely different worlds.

He was raised with happily married parents in the home. And me?

I was a one-night-stand baby.

He was everywhere.

Calling. Texting. Showing up.

And somehow… I got used to it.

He had a way of making himself feel permanent, like he had always been there…

and wasn't going anywhere.

One evening, after a long day of servicing clients and clinicals, he told me to get dressed.

"Why?" I asked.

"Because I said so."

I laughed. "That's not a reason."

"Just trust me."

I rolled my eyes…

but got dressed anyway.

We drove across the city, music playing low. The kind that hums more than it speaks.

He kept glancing over at me, quick looks, like he was checking something… or maybe steadying himself.

Smiling.

But not his usual smile.

"Why do you keep looking at me like that?" I asked.

"Like what?"

"Like you're nervous about something."

He laughed…

but didn't answer.

That's when I started paying attention.

"Where are you taking me? I hope you're not trying to kill me."

He smirked, but still, no answer.

Eventually, we pulled up near the water.

The sky was painted in orange and gold… the kind of sunset that doesn't even look real, like something edited for effect.

Waves crashed softly in the distance, steady and rhythmic.

Everything felt… calm.

Too calm.

He got out first, then walked around and opened my door.

"Okay…" I said slowly, stepping out. "What's going on?"

"Just be patient," he said, smiling, but there it was again. That nervous energy.

"I'm trying," I laughed, but it came out tighter than I expected. "But I don't like surprises… my anxiety is kicking in."

My chest felt a little tight. My mind already trying to fill in blanks that weren't there.

He reached for my hand, warm and steady.

"Calm down… you're safe with me."

Safe.

The word settled somewhere deep in my chest, heavy, unfamiliar… but wanted.

I held onto it as he led me forward.

Then I saw it.

An elegant picnic was set up right on the beach, pillows, soft blankets layered into the sand.

Candles flickered in the breeze. Flowers were placed just right, like someone had adjusted them more than once to get it perfect.

Charcuterie boards sat arranged like something out of a magazine. It didn't even feel real.

Like I had stepped into a movie.

A saxophone played softly in the background. The melody tugged at something in me, familiar.

Happily Ever After by Case.

My heart dropped, heavy, sudden.

It was perfect.

And for a moment… I let myself believe

I deserved this.

That I deserved to be loved like this.

I was already falling.

Before I could even take it all in, he got down on one knee.

Right there in front of me.

He looked up at me like I was everything.

"Maya," he said, his voice steady.

"You know I've been crazy about you since the day I met you."

I just stood there…

frozen.

"You're the strongest woman I know," he continued. "You work harder than anyone I've ever seen."

He paused.

Held my gaze like he needed me to feel every word.

"And I want to build a life with you."

He opened the box.

A diamond ring caught the light—

sharp, blinding.

It shimmered in a way that almost didn't feel real.

"Will you be my forever love?" he said softly. "My wifey…
my everything?"

A breath.

"Marry me."

My heart started racing, fast, uneven.

Everything felt like it was happening too quickly.

Like a dream I didn't want to wake up from.

There was a pause.

So quick most people wouldn't notice it.

But I did.

Something in me… hesitated.

Just for a second.

A small voice, quiet, almost buried.

Asking…

Is this real?

Is this right?

But I pushed it down just as quickly as it came.

Because everything in front of me looked like love.

Felt like love.

Sounded like love.

And I had been waiting for this.

Praying for this.

Wanting this…

For so long.

So, I smiled. Nodded.

And said yes.

His face lit up instantly—

like he already knew what my answer would be.

He stood, pulled me into him, and wrapped his arms around me. Tight. Too tight.

I laughed, a little breathless. "Okay…"

"I told you," he whispered against my ear.

"You were mine. You're stuck with me now," he added, half-joking.

"Am I?" I teased, tilting my head up at him.

He smiled.

But there was something about it… something I couldn't name.

The saxophone kept playing.

The candles flickered.

The ocean moved like nothing in the world had changed.

And maybe it hadn't.

Maybe it was just me.

Overthinking.

Again.

He pulled back and looked at me like I was everything.

Like I was the only thing.

And for a moment…

I let myself stay there—

in that feeling,

in that illusion.

Because everything felt perfect.

I was finally going to live the soft life.

But deep down…

something in me had already started questioning it.

I just wasn't ready to listen yet.

For the first few days, everything felt perfect.

I kept replaying the moment in my head—

the beach,

the music,

the way he looked at me.

I told myself,

This is it.

This is what I've been waiting for.

But it didn't take long…

for things to start feeling familiar again.

One night, not even a week later, he said he was going out.

"With the boys."

I nodded, not thinking too much of it. "Don't be out too late,"
I said, half-joking.

He smirked. "I won't."

But the hours stretched.

My calls went straight to voicemail. My texts… delivered, untouched.

I told myself to ignore it.

He was probably just out. Having fun.

Not glued to his phone. Normal.

Right?

Still, something in me started to tighten, slow at first, then deeper. That same gut feeling…

The one I kept pushing down, like if I ignored it long enough, it would disappear.

By the time I finally fell asleep, it was almost morning.

When I woke up, he still wasn't home.

No message.

No explanation.

Nothing.

I sat there, staring at my phone, my chest heavy with everything I was trying not to name.

Trying not to think the worst.

Trying not to feel what I was already feeling.

Then, hours later…

He walked in.

Like nothing had happened. Like it was just another day.

"You good?" he asked casually, kicking off his shoes.

I looked at him for a second longer than usual.

Too calm. Too normal.

"Yeah," I said.

Because that's what I always said—

even when I wasn't.

CHAPTER 8

The Wedding

The officiant nodded, signaling it was time. Andre went first.

He took my hands in his, held them tight

and looked at me like I was everything.

"I wasn't even looking for this," he began, his voice smooth, steady. "But somehow… you came into my life and changed everything."

Soft murmurs rippled through the crowd.

"You showed me a different kind of love," he continued. "A patient love. A strong love. The kind of love that stays."

My chest tightened, subtle but there.

"I promise to protect you… to stand by you. To build with you… to grow with you." His grip pressed a little firmer around my hands.

"I promise you'll never have to do life alone again."

The words were perfect.

Everything I had ever wanted to hear.

Everything I thought love was supposed to sound like.

I let myself fall into it.

But something about it… didn't fully land.

And instead of questioning it, I questioned myself.

Maybe I was overthinking, like always.

Maybe I was the problem.

Maybe I was so used to things going wrong… I didn't know how to sit inside something good.

The thought rose quietly, uninvited.

I swallowed it.

Buried it.

And smiled through it.

Because everything around me looked like love.

Felt like love.

The officiant turned to me. My turn.

I looked at Andre, and everything slowed.

The ocean behind us blurred into a wash of blue.

The music softened into something distant.

The people watching, gone.

"I didn't come into this looking for perfect," I said softly. "I just wanted something real."

My voice steadied as I spoke.

"And when I met you… I didn't see that right away. But eventually… it grew into something that felt real."

I held his hands a little tighter, grounding myself in the warmth of them.

"I promise to stand beside you… not behind you. To build with you… to grow with you."

A small smile found its way onto my face.

"I promise to love you… even on days it's not easy."

Even on the days it hurts.

I didn't say that part out loud.

"But most of all… I promise to choose you. Every day. As long as we're choosing each other."

The officiant began to speak again, but a sudden gust of wind swept through, sharp and unexpected.

The arch behind us trembled.

Flowers rustled, petals lifting and shifting like something unsettled in the air.

Candles flickered, one going out completely. No one said anything.

A few people smiled it off. But I noticed.

I glanced at the candle a second longer than I should have… then looked back at him.

And smiled.

Like everything was still perfect.

That night… everything was supposed to feel official. I was his wife now.

The room was quiet when we got back. Soft lighting.

Flowers from earlier still arranged around the room, like the day was trying to hold on a little longer.

I kicked off my shoes, letting out a small breath.

"Today was beautiful," I said, smiling.

He watched me.

Not the same way he had earlier. Something about his energy felt… different.

"Yeah," he said. "It was."

A pause settled between us.

Then he walked over and pulled me in. Kissing me.

Caressing me. Moving with a kind of urgency that felt unfamiliar.

Doing things…

we had never done before.

I froze for a second.

"Relax," he said softly. "It's okay."

I nodded.

Trying to match his energy.

Trying not to make it awkward.

Trying not to feel… confused.

This wasn't us.

Or at least, it wasn't the version of us I thought I knew.

I let out a small laugh, brushing it off.

"You switching things up on me now?" I teased, keeping my tone light.

He smirked.

"Something like that."

But there was something behind that smile.

And instead of asking questions…

I adjusted.

Went along with it.

Like I always did.

Telling myself, maybe this is normal.

He turned me over, reaching for the oil. I felt it spill, warm against my skin, trailing down slowly.

His hands followed, spreading it, moving with intention, firmer now, more controlled.

Then suddenly—

I tensed. My body reacting before my mind could catch up.

I jerked slightly.

"Relax," he said again. "You trust me, right?"

I nodded.

But something inside me had already started to pull back.

The next moment happened too fast.

A sharp, overwhelming pressure, and then pain.

A scream tore out of me before I could stop it. A sound I didn't recognize as my own.

It felt like my body was being split open.

I tried to move, to get away, but he held me down.

One hand forced both of my wrists together.

The other pressed hard against the back of my neck.

I couldn't move.

The pain was blinding. Consuming. Nothing I had ever felt before.

My thoughts scattered.

I tried to breathe through it.

Tried to think of something, anything else.

But it didn't work.

And then…

something shifted.

My body responded in a way my mind couldn't understand. Sensations blurring together, pain and something else, something confusing, something I didn't have words for.

I felt overwhelmed. Disoriented.

Like I was no longer fully inside myself.

A thought flickered through my mind

Is this what they mean when they say pain and pleasure are the same?

Before I could make sense of it, he pulled away.

Turned me around.

His grip moved to my head, firm, controlling.

"Open your mouth," he said.

"I want you to taste me." He tried to force himself into my mouth, but I gagged.

"Open your throat," he said, yanking my head back, pushing

deeper despite my reaction.

"Okay," I whispered, my voice barely there.

Moments later, it was over. I felt it on my face, in my mouth, something I hadn't prepared myself for.

A heaviness settled in my chest.

I felt small. Used. Like I had been reduced to something I didn't recognize, something transactional, detached from who I believed I was. The thought made my stomach turn.

I went straight to the bathroom. Washed my face. Spit, over and over, like I could get the feeling out of me. My mouth felt numb, unfamiliar, like it didn't belong to me.

I scrubbed my tongue harder than necessary. Brushed longer than I ever had before.

But the feeling didn't leave.

Lower down, the burning wouldn't ease either, so I ran a bath and lowered myself into the water, hoping it would soothe something, anything.

The next morning…

I woke up before him. The room was quiet.

Sunlight slipped through the curtains, soft and warm, too gentle for how I felt. Like nothing had shifted. Like everything was still perfect.

I lay there, staring at the ceiling.

Replaying the night before.

Not all of it.

Just certain moments. The ones that didn't sit right. The ones that felt… unfamiliar.

I shifted slightly, glancing over at him. He was still asleep. Peaceful. Undisturbed.

I started questioning myself.

Maybe I was overthinking again.

Maybe I was making something out of nothing. Maybe this was normal.

People grow.

People try new things… right?

I exhaled slowly and turned away, pressing the thoughts down before they could fully form. I covered them with logic, anything to make it make sense.

I had just said "I do."

I didn't want to believe that something could already feel off.

So, I got up.

Walked into the bathroom. Stood in front of the mirror.

"Everything is fine," I whispered.

I forced a small smile.

And for a moment…

I believed it.

CHAPTER 9

Marriage Life

Not long after the wedding… I got pregnant.

And motherhood… changed everything.

My priorities didn't shift gradually, they flipped overnight.

It wasn't just about me anymore.

I was still working as an advanced esthetician… still in school, still doing clinicals for my degree… and now,

raising a baby.

My life didn't slow down. If anything…

it sped up.

Days blurred into nights. Feedings, assignments, clients, exhaustion, I was moving constantly, barely pausing long enough to feel anything.

He promised he would help. And sometimes…

he did.

Sometimes he showed up. Held the baby like he meant it. Stayed present.

And I held onto those moments, tight.

Because they made everything else easier to excuse.

But other times…

he disappeared.

At first, it was small. Late nights.

"With the boys." Random weekends. "I'm just kicking it."

And I told myself not to make it a thing. Everybody needs space.

Time with their friends.

I didn't want to be that woman, the one always questioning, always accusing.

I didn't want to seem toxic.

So I stayed quiet.

Even when something in me pressed against my chest, asking to be heard.

But over time…

it started happening more.

The drinking picked up.

And when he drank… something about him shifted.

The way he looked at me, like I was an inconvenience instead of someone he chose.

His energy. His tone.

The man I married…

started to feel like someone I didn't recognize.

He would come home drunk.

Eat. Sleep.

And sometimes…

start arguments over nothing.

Small things would turn into big ones. The way I said something, a tone I didn't even realize I had, would set him off.

And somehow, it always came back to me.

"You always tripping."

"You're insecure."

"You doing too much."

The words didn't just land, they stayed.

And after hearing them enough…

they started to sound like truth.

Maybe I was the problem.

Maybe I was too sensitive.

Maybe I didn't know how to just be happy.

So I adjusted.

I shrank where I could.

Spoke less.

Questioned myself before I ever questioned him.

Because at the time…

that felt easier than losing him. I shrunk myself.

Watched what I said. Watched how I said it. Tried to stay soft.

Tried to stay easy.

Tried not to trigger anything.

Because I never knew what version of him I was going to get.

So, I did what I always did—

I tried to keep the peace.

For the baby.

For the family I had worked so hard to create.

Because it wasn't just about me anymore. It was bigger than me.

And I told myself,

This is what a marriage goes through. For better or for worse.

This is what commitment looks like.

But deep down...

that feeling came back.

The one I had spent my whole life ignoring, quiet, persistent, uncomfortable.

Telling me something wasn't right.

Still...

I pushed it down. Called it stress. Called it hormones. Called it a phase.

Because the truth...

felt heavier than anything I was ready to carry.

And the last thing I wanted to believe...

was that I wasn't overthinking.

That I wasn't the problem.

That everything I was trying so hard to hold together...

was already falling apart.

CHAPTER 10

The First Fight

The first real fight we had… it started over something small. It always does.

He had been gone for two days.

No calls. No texts. Nothing.

I sat at the kitchen table feeding my baby, forcing my hands to stay steady… pretending it didn't bother me.

Pretending I was calm.

Then I heard the front door open.

He walked in like nothing had happened. Like two days meant nothing.

He smelled like alcohol…

like smoke…

like somewhere I wasn't supposed to know about.

"Where have you been?" I asked.

My voice came out calm, but my chest was already tightening.

He shrugged. "Out.

"For two days?"

"Relax."

And just like that… I felt it.

That familiar pressure creeping up my chest, thick and

suffocating.

"You're a husband and a father now," I said. "You can't just disappear like that."

He rolled his eyes.

"I told you I was with the boys."

"You didn't tell me shit," I said, the words slipping out sharper than I meant.

"Are you fucking your boys? You spend more time with them than you do your own family."

His whole energy shifted.

Louder.

Sharper.

"Bitch, are you calling me gay? How dare you disrespect me like"

"Bitch? Who the fuck are you calling a bitch?" I snapped, my voice rising before I could stop it.

"You're always claiming you're with them like they matter more than your own family."

"Why are you always questioning me about everything?" he shot back.

"If I breathe wrong, you're questioning me."

I stood up from the table, my body tense, trying to hold everything in.

"Because I care," I said. "And I'm the one here taking care of our responsibilities."

He let out a bitter laugh.

"Oh, here we go again."

"What does that mean?"

"You acting like you do everything."

"I do."

That's when it shifted.

He slammed his hand against the counter, hard.

The sound cracked through the kitchen, sharp enough to make me flinch.

"You think you're better than me," he said. "Because of your little degrees... your little fucking businesses... you're fake as fuck... a fake bitch."

His words didn't just land, they stung, sharp and sudden, like a slap I didn't see coming.

"Oh, so now I'm fake?" I let out a laugh, but it came out thinner than I meant it to. "I wasn't fake when you were pursuing me. You knew who I was when you married me."

"Yeah," he said. "But I didn't know you were a fake-ass bitch. And now you want to call me gay."

"That's not what I said."

But it didn't matter. The damage had already settled in the room, thick and unmoving.

"You really think I don't do anything around here? That I

don't help you out?" he said.

"I made your life easier so you could work and go to school. Who was there? Who was cooking? Cleaning? Holding things down so you could focus?"

I let out a breath, shaking my head. "Did I ask you to? I remember managing everything on my own… and even more now, with a baby tied to my hip."

"I supported you," he pushed. "I made it easier for you to be who you are."

I shook my head again, slower this time.

"No," I said, my voice quieter, but steadier. "I became who I am because I had to… before you were even in my life."

A pause settled between us. Heavy. Pressing.

"You were there sometimes," I added. "But don't confuse support… with sacrifice."

He laughed, sharp, dismissive.

"Oh, so now it's 'sometimes'?"

"You really think, in that big-ass head of yours, that you did all this by yourself?" he said.

"Yes!" I snapped, the word tearing out of me before I could soften it. "You're never here. Fuck you."

He turned and stormed out. The door slammed so hard it rattled the walls.

And just like that… he was gone. Again.

I stood there in the kitchen, my baby still in my arms, her weight grounding me while everything else felt like it was slipping.

The silence crept in slowly, filling every corner of the room.

And for the first time since the wedding… a thought pushed its way through—

What if I made a mistake?

My chest tightened.

I swallowed it down. Fast.

Because I didn't come this far… didn't fight this hard… didn't build all of this… just for it to fall apart.

Not now.

Not yet.

CHAPTER 11

The Disappearances

At first…

I told myself I was overthinking. He had always been social.

Always liked being around people being out, being seen.

But lately…

the time he spent away from home started changing.

It became random. Quiet. Secretive.

What used to be a few hours out with his friends…

turned into overnight.

Then days.

One Friday evening…

I was lying on the couch, my baby asleep on my chest, her tiny breaths warm against my skin. The house was too quiet, the kind of quiet that makes every thought louder.

He had left the night before.

Said he was going to meet his boys.

That was almost thirty hours ago.

No calls. No texts.

I stared at my phone, turning it over in my hand like it might suddenly come alive.

My mind wouldn't stop—

Should I call again?

Should I just leave it alone?

I had already called multiple times earlier. Straight to voicemail.

A tight feeling settled in my chest.

Did he turn off his phone…

or did he block me?

Finally, the front door opened.

My body went still before I could even think.

He walked in like nothing had happened.

Like he had just stepped out for a few minutes.

"Where have you been?" I asked.

He kicked off his shoes. "Out."

"For almost two days?"

He shrugged.

Like it wasn't a big deal.

Like time didn't matter.

Like I was the problem for asking.

"Why are you questioning me? I'm not your child… you don't run shit but your mouth," he said.

"I'm not questioning you," I said, my voice quieter than I expected. "I just want to know where my husband disappears to for days. I was worried."

He walked to the fridge, grabbed a bottle of water, and twisted it open. He didn't even look at me.

"I told you, "He said. "I was with the boys."

Something about the way he said it… it shut the conversation down. Final. Like there was nothing left to ask. Like I was supposed to take it, swallow it, and move on.

But this time… I didn't.

I watched him, really watched him. The way he moved. The way his voice dragged slightly when he spoke.

His eyes were bloodshot.

His movements… off. Slower than usual. Almost delayed.

Then I noticed the smell.

Alcohol, yes. Sharp and familiar.

But underneath it… something else. Something I couldn't place yet.

Not yet.

But I would.

And when I did…

There would be no unseeing it.

PART IV – CRACKS IN THE MARRIAGE

CHAPTER 12

The Devil's Powder

The first time I saw the addiction for what it really was… didn't happen inside our home.

It happened at a party.

Andre had been invited to an all-white party. I didn't know the birthday person.

Didn't know the crowd. But he kept pushing.

"Just come out with me tonight," he said. "I want to show you off."

Something in me hesitated…

…but I went anyway.

When I got dressed, I took my time.

My makeup was flawless, soft, but defined in all the right places. My hair, short and curled just right, framed my face perfectly. My body was snatched… curvy in all the ways I knew how to be.

The white lace dress hugged every inch of me. It stopped just three inches under my butt, fitting like it had been made for me. Lifting what it needed to. Accentuating what it should.

My skin glowed, that soft, golden shimmer against my caramel tone… like I was lit from within. My legs looked long, smooth, and shining under the lights.

On my feet, my white Yves Saint Laurent heels, the logo sitting bold right at the front.

I looked good. I smelled good. No…

I looked like it was my birthday. Like I was the party.

And I felt it.

The club was packed when we got there, everybody dressed in white. The music was loud, vibrating through my chest. Drinks and hookah smoke filled the air, thick and sweet.

The energy felt chaotic… almost overwhelming.

Andre lit up the moment we walked in.

Dapping people up. Hugging strangers. Moving fast.

Introducing me from person to person—

"This my wife," he kept saying.

But the introductions didn't last.

Within minutes… he disappeared.

At first, I told myself it was nothing.

It's a party. Just have fun. Don't overthink it.

Let him do what he do.

Let him enjoy himself.

It's a party.

Maybe he went to the bar.

Maybe the bathroom.

But minutes stretched…

and stretched…

until it had been almost an hour.

And I was still sitting there, smoking hookah alone, watching everyone else laugh, dance, exist like they didn't have a care in the world. Like time wasn't dragging on me personally.

I kept my eyes moving, pretending I wasn't waiting for anything in particular.

That's when one of the men Andre had introduced me to earlier slid into the seat beside me. At least… I think he was one of his friends. I'd never seen him before. Truthfully, I hadn't really seen any of them before, just faces passing through Andre's world.

He leaned in like we shared history.

Then he placed his hand on my lap. "You Andre's girl, right?"

I looked at his hand first, then at him.

"His wife," I said, moving his hand off me.

He smirked like I hadn't corrected him at all. "Yeah… I heard about you."

Something about the way he said it didn't sit right. His eyes didn't just look at me, they moved over me, slow, deliberate, like he was trying to read something I hadn't said out loud.

Then he shook his head. "Damn… you fine. You too good for him."

My stomach tightened instantly.

"What the fuck does that mean?" I asked, sharper than I

intended. "And what exactly have you heard about me?"

He shrugged like I was overreacting.

"I'm just saying… if you were mine, things would be different."

I went still.

Not because it was flattering. Because it didn't land like flirting. It felt calculated, like he was placing something in the air on purpose and watching to see how I'd breathe through it.

"You a good woman," he added, eyes still on me in a way that felt too steady. "Everybody knows that."

My brows pulled together. "Everybody?"

"Yeah," he said with a small smirk. "Word gets around."

There was a pause after that, one that stretched too long.

My chest tightened, quiet but unmistakable.

"What kind of word?" I asked, trying to sound casual. It didn't come out casual.

He leaned back a little, like this was nothing. Too nothing.

"Just that you hold things down," he said. "You loyal. You solid."

I didn't smile.

"How do you even know Andre?" I asked, more direct now.

That smirk returned, like he'd been waiting for that question.

"Oh, we go way back," he said. "Same circles… same people."

He gave a short, dry laugh.

Something in my chest shifted, irritation, suspicion, both tangled together.

"Say what you're trying to say," I said, voice tightening. "I don't speak in code."

He lifted his hands slightly, almost amused. "I'm just saying you're a good woman."

But I couldn't let it go.

I kept hearing his words again in my head, that's a good woman right there, like it meant something different in his mouth than it should have.

Not praise.

Not respect.

Something else.

Something heavier.

Something that made the space around us feel smaller than it was a minute ago. I scooted a little farther away from him, like space alone could reset whatever was building in my chest.

I tried to shake the feeling off, but when I finally looked up, I realized people had been watching us. Not openly, never openly. Just those lingering glances that stick too long before snapping away the second you notice them. Whispered conversations half-hidden behind hands.

My chest tightened.

I scanned the room again, searching for Andre.

"How would my husband feel about you flirting with his wife?" I asked, my voice sharper than I intended.

"He won't mind," he said with an easy smile, like the question didn't even land. Like it was nothing.

Something in me snapped quiet instead of loud.

"I'm going to find my husband," I said, standing up before I could second-guess myself.

I moved through the club, weaving between bodies and noise and flashing lights that felt too close, too heavy. I checked every corner, every cluster of people.

Nothing.

Outside, I finally stepped away from the crowd. The music dulled behind me, but my body still felt like it was vibrating from it. The night air was cooler against my skin, softer, but it didn't settle me the way I needed it to.

That anxious feeling in my chest stayed right where it was.

I pulled out my phone. No messages. No missed calls. Nothing from him.

My brows pulled together as I looked around again, like maybe I'd just missed him somehow.

Then I saw him. Down the street.

Andre.

Standing with two guys… and three girls. Laughing. Talking

like he had all the time in the world. Like nothing was missing. Like I wasn't.

Something about the scene didn't sit right in my body. Too easy. Too familiar.

One of the girls touched his arm like it belonged there. Like she'd done it before.

And he didn't flinch. Didn't shift away. Didn't even look like it crossed his mind to. He just smiled.

That same smile. The one I knew. The one I thought was mine.

My stomach dropped so fast it felt like the ground had moved.

I stood there, frozen for a second, watching him like I was looking at someone I thought I knew… and realizing I might not have known him at all.

Or maybe I did. And I just refused to see it.

One of the girls leaned in closer and said something that made him throw his head back laughing. The sound hit me wrong, too loud, too carefree, too easy.

Something in me tightened. Irritation. Hurt. Confusion all tangled together until I couldn't separate them anymore.

Everything about him in that moment felt unfamiliar.

I whispered under my breath, more to myself than anything, "this man really got me messed up."

And before I could stop myself, before I could think through what I was about to walk into… I started moving toward them.

Each step heavier than the last.

The closer I got, the louder their laughter became. The more my chest tightened. The more my thoughts started racing ahead of me.

One of the girls noticed me first. Her expression shifted, barely. Subtle. Controlled.

But I saw it.

Then the others turned.

One by one… until I finally saw Andre.

His eyes met mine, and I could tell immediately, I'd irritated him.

Like I'd interrupted something I wasn't supposed to step into.

"Hey…" I said, keeping my voice steady. "There you are." It sounded normal enough.

But I wasn't normal. I was irritated… pissed.

He glanced at the group first, then back at me. "What you doing out here?" he asked.

Not are you okay.

Not I was looking for you.

Just, what you doing out here.

I forced a small smile. "I was looking for you."

A beat.

One of the girls shifted beside him, her arm still too close to his. Too comfortable.

"Yeah, I just stepped out for a minute," he said quickly, then added, "You good though?"

You good.

Like I was the one out of place.

Like I was the one interrupting something I didn't belong in.

I looked at him. Then at them. Then back at him.

"I'm good," I said.

And the strange part… I was good.

Like my emotions had gone quiet just long enough for everything to sharpen.

And what I saw was simple.

I wasn't being introduced.

Wasn't being acknowledged.

Wasn't being claimed.

I was just… there.

Standing in front of my husband, feeling like a stranger.

"I'm ready to go," I told him.

He barely looked at me. "I'm not ready yet."

"What?"

"I'm about to go back inside and dance."

I held his gaze, waiting for something to shift. It didn't.

This… didn't feel normal.

But I didn't argue. I didn't want to make a scene. So, I followed him back inside.

And he wasn't the same anymore.

Standing on couches.

Drinking nonstop.

Smoking cigarettes, something he knew I hated.

Moving through the crowd like he couldn't stay still, like something inside him had loosened and taken over.

It scared me.

I grabbed his arm. "I'm leaving," I said. "Come on."

He looked agitated… but eventually followed me out.

The drive home was silent.

But my chest stayed heavy the entire way. I couldn't shake it.

When we got home, I went straight upstairs. I needed a shower, needed to wash that night off me, like I could rinse away what I'd just seen and felt.

But under the water, I froze.

Voices. Downstairs. Multiple voices.

My heart dropped so fast it felt like it hit my stomach.

I shut the water off in a panic, my hands already shaking before I even realized it. I threw on pajamas, barely thinking, and walked downstairs.

And there they were.

Standing in my living room like they belonged there.

The same girls from outside. Three of them.

And two of his friends.

Like my house was just open access.

Rage hit me so quickly it burned.

"Who the fuck are y'all and what the fuck are y'all doing in my house?!" I yelled.

Silence.

"Get the fuck out. Now!"

"Right now!"

They didn't even move fast.

That slow response made something twist harder in my chest, like I was the one interrupting something that belonged to them.

One of the girls laughed under her breath. Then another followed. Low, whispered, but still loud enough for me to hear.

Like I was overreacting. Like this wasn't even my home.

I stood there trying to make sense of it, trying to catch up to what I was seeing.

How did I go from wife… to a stranger in my own space?

I turned to Andre.

"Have you lost your damn mind?" I snapped. "You bringing strangers into my house where my kids sleep?"

He didn't even flinch the way I expected him to. He just looked at me, annoyed.

Like I was the problem. Like I was embarrassing him.

One of the guys shook his head, half-smiling.

"Aight, man, we gone," he said, dapping Andre up like this

was normal. "We'll catch you later."

Andre nodded.

Unbothered.

Like I wasn't even standing there.

The girls moved slowly, still giggling, still whispering like I was entertainment instead of a human being in my own home.

One of them looked me up and down before turning away.

And just like that, they left.

I turned back to Andre.

He barely reacted.

"My bad," he muttered, already turning away like it didn't matter.

Then he went upstairs.

I stood there shaking, alone in the middle of my own living room.

When he came back down, he acted like nothing had happened.

"The homie tire burst and they stranded on the freeway," he said.

I just stared at him.

"What that got to do with you?" he snapped. "He don't have Triple A."

"What?" he yelled again. "No, and I'm not about to leave the homie stranded. I'm going to use our membership, and I have to be there to show my ID."

I stared at him, feeling it in my gut, that everything he was saying sounded rehearsed, off, like a lie he was trying to sell me and himself at the same time.

"You're drunk. You're not taking my car, especially not after you just totaled yours… and I still don't even know what really happened."

He exhaled hard through his nose, like I was the problem. "Fine."

Then he turned and went back upstairs, already on his phone like the conversation didn't matter.

Eventually, I fell asleep on the couch, exhausted in a way that wasn't just physical. It was the kind of tired that sits behind your eyes, heavy and emotional, like your body is still awake even when you're not.

Sometime later… I woke up to the sound of my front door closing.

A car pulled off outside.

I shot up immediately.

My heart started racing before my feet even hit the floor.

I ran to the door and pulled it open.

It was unlocked.

He had left it like that, like my home was something anyone could walk into while I was sleeping alone.

My car was gone.

I grabbed my purse.

Keys, gone.

Money, gone.

A cold panic started crawling up my chest.

I called his phone over and over.

No answer.

The silence on the other end made it worse.

Panic fully set in now.

I called a friend.

We drove around all night looking for him, street after street, gas stations, corners I didn't even recognize anymore. Nothing.

By the time morning came, I still hadn't heard from him.

I called his aunt. She had the baby.

She hadn't heard from him either.

"I'm coming to get you," she said.

But right as her car pulled into the driveway… he showed up behind her.

My stomach dropped.

My heart started pounding so hard it felt like it was pushing against my throat.

The engine cut.

The door opened.

And he stepped out.

His movements were slow, delayed, like his body was there but everything else was lagging behind it.

His eyes were low.

Glossy.

Not fully present.

He looked at me…

but it didn't feel like he saw me.

"Why you calling everybody getting them in our business?" he asked, like I was the problem.

No urgency.

No explanation.

No concern.

Just irritation.

I stared at him for a second, trying to read him.

Trying to make sense of it.

"Where the fuck were you with my car?" I asked.

He shrugged.

Like the answer didn't matter.

"Out."

That was it. Out.

Like hours hadn't passed.

Like I hadn't been sitting there, waiting.

Mind running in circles, landing on the worst every time.

Behind me, his aunt stepped out of the car, watching quietly.

Even she could feel it, that shift in the air.

Something wasn't right.

But he stood there… unbothered.

Like the chaos he caused only existed in my head.

His aunt stepped forward.

"Where have you been, Andre?" she asked, her voice firm.

He didn't look at her right away.

Just let out a slow breath, irritated.

"I'm straight, Aunt," he muttered.

Like that answered anything.

Something in me snapped.

"You ain't fucking straight," I said, my voice rising before I could stop it. "You been gone in my car, took my money, and that's all you got to say?"

I shook my head. "I already know what you been doing."

He looked at me then. Finally.

Eyes low. Expression flat.

"What are you talking about now?" he said, almost amused.

A dry laugh slipped out of me.

"Don't play with me. You was just with them same bitches you brought into my house."

Silence stretched between us.

"I wasn't with them," he said calmly.

Too calmly.

I shook my head, stepping back, needing space I didn't have.

"I'm done," I said. "I want a divorce. Right now."

And just like that, he flipped.

His face hardened, something sharp settling in his eyes.

"So now you just making shit up?" he snapped. "You always do this. Always assuming, thinking you know everything."

"You always tripping."

"You always got something negative to say." His words came faster now, piling on top of each other. "Running around putting people in our fucking business, acting crazy, embarrassing me…"

Embarrassing him.

I stared at him, the words ringing in my ears.

Trying to understand how it turned so fast.

How I went from asking a question… to being the problem.

His aunt stepped closer, studying him this time, really studying him.

Then she paused.

Her whole expression shifted. "What's that on your nose…"

She leaned in slightly, her voice dropping.

"He ain't right. He on that shit."

White residue.

He wiped his nose quickly, like it wasn't there.

And suddenly… everything clicked.

The way he'd been looking through me instead of at me.

The distance. The coldness.

This wasn't just him being dismissive.

This was something deeper.

And just like that… everything exploded.

He started breaking things, the table,

the TV, anything he could get his hands on.

The sound of things shattering filled the room, sharp and sudden.

Then he turned toward me.

Not just looking, squaring up. Like he wanted to fight.

My chest tightened. I couldn't move.

His aunt stepped in between us before he could get any closer.

"Pack you a bag," she said, firm now. "We're leaving. Right now."

I didn't argue. I didn't think.

I just moved.

Grabbed what I could. Left the rest behind.

And we were gone.

I stayed away for a week.

But that night… wasn't the end.

It was the beginning.

CHAPTER 13

The Promise of Change

After that night… nothing was the same.

I stayed at my friend's house for a week.

Trying to think. Trying to breathe.

Trying to make sense of everything, but my mind wouldn't stop.

It kept replaying it. Over and over.

The drugs. The lies.

Those bitches standing in my house like they belonged there.

The sound of things breaking.

And the look in his eyes… when he lost control.

That look stayed with me. It followed me into quiet moments, into sleep, into the spaces where I just wanted silence.

Part of me wanted to leave. For good.

But another part of me…

kept reaching back.

Remembering who he used to be.

The man who cooked for me after long days.

The man who celebrated me like my wins were his.

The man who used to look at me… like I was everything.

And that part of me?

Wouldn't let go.

When I finally went back home… he was there.

And something about him felt different.

Not his appearance.

Not his voice.

His energy.

He looked… defeated.

Tired. Ashamed.

Like something in him had finally cracked open.

"I messed up," he said quietly.

I didn't respond.

"I know I did."

I crossed my arms, holding myself tighter than I needed to.

"So, what now?"

He sat down on the couch like the weight of everything was finally catching up to him.

"I can't keep living like this."

"You think I can?" I shot back.

He rubbed his face, slow and heavy.

Like he didn't even recognize himself anymore.

"I need a fresh start."

I almost laughed.

Not because it was funny…

but because I had heard that before.

But this time…

something in his voice felt different.

Desperate.

"Let's move," he said.

I blinked.

"Move where?"

"Another state."

I stared at him. "You're serious?"

He nodded.

"If I stay here… I'm going to keep running into the same people. The same temptations. The same lifestyle."

He leaned forward, like he needed me to really hear him.

"If we leave… I can change."

I stayed quiet.

Because I didn't know what to believe anymore.

"You can open another business," he continued. "You always figure things out."

"And you?" I asked.

He didn't hesitate. "I'll stay clean. I'll focus on my family."

A pause. Then softer, "I'll be the husband you deserve."

And that's the moment that broke me.

Because I wanted to believe him.

Not a little. Not halfway.

I wanted to believe him completely.

But still…

there was this small voice inside me, barely above a whisper:

What if moving finally fixes us?

Maybe it wasn't him.

Maybe it was the environment. The people.

The access.

Maybe if we left it all behind… we could finally be okay.

I told him I needed time to think it over, but I also needed him to be sober.

He checked into rehab. Started going to AA.

Two months passed.

He kept his word. Stayed sober.

For a while, I felt like I had the old Andre back, the loving, caring version of him I missed so much.

But then…

he started disappearing again.

Coming back high.

Angry. Paranoid.

Breaking things. Picking fights over nothing.

And when the high wore off, he would crash.

"I hate myself," he'd say.

"I don't want to live like this."

And me?

I felt sorry for him.

I tried everything. Rehab. Meetings. Counseling. Therapy.

Anything that could save him. Save us.

But nothing worked.

He would stay sober for a little while… and then slip right back into it.

Like something always pulling him under.

Until one day…

he came to me begging.

"Let's move," he said. "To another state."

"Somewhere I don't know anybody. I need a fresh start."

I looked at him. Really looked at him.

The man I loved… was slipping away right in front of me.

And his secrets… his addiction…

they were catching up to him.

But I still wanted my husband back.

I still believed in our marriage.

I had already poured everything into saving us. Counseling.

Rehab. Meetings. Therapy. Money.

Time. Energy. Love.

Everything I had.

And still… nothing worked.

So I made a decision.

The hardest one I had ever made.

I said yes.

I sold my business.

The business I built from nothing.

The one that gave me independence.

The one that made me feel like me.

I let it go.

And with that money… I bought us a house.

In another state.

A fresh start.

A clean slate.

A new life.

For us.

For our family.

For the man I still believed was in there somewhere.

But what I didn't understand then…

what I refused to see…

was this:

You can run from people.

You can run from places.

But you cannot run from truth.

And Andre's truth…

wasn't tied to a location.

It was inside him.

Waiting.

CHAPTER 14

A New House

The new house was beautiful, bigger than anything we had before. High ceilings.

Wide windows.

Sunlight poured into every room, soft and forgiving, like it was trying to convince me this was real.

A quiet neighborhood…

the kind where kids rode bikes in the street, and neighbors actually waved when you passed by.

Exactly what he said we needed.

A fresh start.

And for a while, it felt like one.

He stayed home more. Helped with the kids.

Even cooked dinner sometimes… like he used to in the beginning.

I let myself believe it.

I had my husband back.

Meanwhile…

I was rebuilding everything I gave up.

New clients.

Networking events.

Long days.

Balancing motherhood, work… and finishing my master's program.

Laying the foundation for my future medical spa.

Starting over wasn't easy.

But I had never been afraid of starting over. I'd done it too many times before.

I knew how to build.

That's who I was.

But slowly…

things started slipping.

At first, it was small.

Late nights here and there. The same excuses.

"I'll be back in a few hours."

Then hours turned into nights.

And nights…

turned into mornings.

The same distance.

Different place… same patterns.

I felt it before I admitted it, that familiar tightening in my chest, that quiet knowing I kept trying to silence.

That feeling came back.

The one I tried so hard to ignore.

And that's when it hit me.

Not all at once…

but steady enough that I couldn't pretend anymore.

I had been bamboozled.

It was never the location.

Never the people.

No matter where we went… nothing changed.

Because his addictions didn't follow him, they lived in him.

He was the addiction.

The party.

The connection.

The one everybody gravitated toward.

The one that pulled everything in.

He was the birthday cake…

and everybody just wanted a turn to blow out the candle.

And me?

I was still standing there…

Trying to build a life with someone

who was being shared with the world.

One night—

I heard the front door open.

3 a.m.

I had been awake the entire time.

But when I heard his footsteps coming toward the bedroom…

I closed my eyes.

Pretending to be asleep.

I didn't want to argue.

Didn't want to fight.

Didn't want another conversation that led nowhere.

I felt him enter the room, moving slowly,

carefully, like he was trying not to exist.

Then I heard it.

The zipper of my purse.

My heart started pounding, hard, fast, loud enough I was sure he could hear it.

I cracked my eyes open just enough to see.

He looked over at me.

Checking.

Making sure I was still "asleep."

Then he reached into my purse.

Pulled out cash.

Then my debit card.

Something inside me snapped.

But I stayed still.

Watching.

Waiting.

He turned and walked toward the door.

And the second he stepped into the hallway—

I jumped up.

Ran straight to my purse.

Just to make sure I wasn't tripping.

Money gone.

Card gone.

My chest tightened.

I didn't even think.

I just reacted.

I ran outside.

He was halfway into an Uber.

"Andre!" I yelled.

He looked at me, and still started getting into the car.

I stepped in front of it, so they couldn't drive off.

"Get your ass out right now!" I yelled.

He got out, already trying to push past me.

I grabbed him by his shirt

and swung him with everything in me.

He stumbled, too drunk, too high,

too far gone to even catch himself.

He hit the pavement hard.

I reached into his pockets and pulled out my money.

My card.

"Yo, stupid ass is stealing from me now?" I snapped.

He barely reacted.

His eyes… empty.

Glassy.

Like he wasn't even there.

Lost.

Not knowing what was going on.

And that hurt more than anything.

Because the man I loved, he wasn't in those eyes anymore.

Just a stranger staring back at me.

Something in me snapped.

I kicked him.

Hard.

"Get your fucking life together," I said, and I walked away.

I didn't look back.

Didn't care if he got up.

Didn't care where he went.

Because this wasn't just addiction anymore.

This was betrayal.

Disrespect.

Survival.

Behind me…

I heard the car door shut.

And just like that,

he disappeared again.

CHAPTER 15

The Bridge

Days passed, no calls, no texts, no sign of him.

And this time, I didn't go looking.

I stayed focused on what I could actually control, my work, my clients, my kids, my future. I refused to let his chaos spill back into my life the way it used to. Something in me had shifted, even if no one else could see it.

But I could feel it.

I stopped caring in the way I used to.

I wasn't checking on him anymore. I wasn't trying to decode him, predict him, or make sense of him. I just let him move how he moved, without me in the middle of it.

Then my phone buzzed while I was at work.

A group message.

His family. All of them, the ones he stayed close with.

And then the messages started rolling in, one after another.

"I'm tired of living like this."

"Nobody loves me."

"No one understands me."

"Everyone hates me."

"My wife hates me."

Then—

"I think it's time I do everyone a favor."

"I'm about to jump off the bridge."

I stared at the screen.

And just like that, the panic spread through the thread.

"Where are you??"

"Stop playing!"

"Answer the phone!"

Then someone tagged me.

"Maya please talk to him."

I was sitting in my treatment room with a client in front of me, the weight of it pressing into the space like it had its own body.

And I just… exhaled.

Not because I didn't feel anything.

Because I had.

I had seen this before. Not once, but multiple times.

But for them, this was the first time witnessing it.

Every time he needed attention, or felt guilty, or wanted me to come running, it was always the same pattern.

Same script. Different day.

Now with his family pulled into it. That part was new for him.

He hated when they saw anything negative about him. He needed to stay perfect in their eyes.

Perfect wife.

Perfect house.

Perfect life.

My phone kept buzzing nonstop.

"Maya, please call him."

"You're the only one he listens to."

"He needs you."

What they didn't understand was simple, he didn't just want help. He wanted me.

And I was tired.

So, I typed back,

"I'm with a client right now. I can't deal with this."

His mom called next.

"Maya... can you please go check on my son? He's not answering any of my calls... please..."

I agreed.

Not because I believed the pani, but because if he really did something to himself, I knew I'd carry that weight.

I asked my assistant to finish the session, grabbed my keys, and left.

The drive home felt longer than it should have.

When I got there, the door was unlocked.

The house was quiet in that heavy, unnatural way that makes your chest tighten before you even understand why.

I called his name.

No answer.

I called again.

Still nothing.

The third time, my voice came out sharper, frustrated now, not just worried.

This time, he picked up.

"I'm at the bridge," he said.

His voice was calm, but it wasn't peace. It was emptiness. Like something in him had already shut down.

I didn't argue. I didn't ask questions.

I just got in the car and drove.

When I pulled up, I saw him.

Sitting on the side rail like he had been waiting for me all along.

When he got into the car, I barely recognized him.

The smell hit me first, sweat, alcohol, something stale I couldn't place.

His eyes looked heavy. Yellowed. Off.

His ankle was swollen.

And then he started talking.

"I feel like nobody cares about me…"

I kept my eyes on the road. I didn't respond.

I'd heard this before. Same words. Same tears. Same promises that never held past the moment they were spoken.

Different city, different state, same cycle.

We kept moving, thinking distance might change something. But it never did. It wasn't the places. It was him. It had always been him.

Instead of heading home, I turned into a hotel parking lot.

He looked at me, confused. "You're not coming home?"

"No."

I checked him into a room quietly, like I was trying not to wake something already half-dead inside both of us. I took his phone. His wallet. His clothes.

Left him there with water. Food. A space where he could come down safely without falling apart somewhere I couldn't pull him back from.

"I'll check on you tomorrow," I said.

He didn't argue. He couldn't. He was too far gone for resistance.

As I walked back to my car, something inside me shifted, quiet, final, like a door closing without a sound.

I stopped believing I could save him.

Because love isn't enough.

Not when someone is committed to destroying themselves from the inside out.

And for the first time since all of this began, I let myself think it without taking it back:

Maybe I need to leave.

PART V – THE TRUTH BEHIND THE LIES

CHAPTER 16

Living on Guard

After I left him in that hotel room, something in me shifted.

It wasn't loud. It didn't happen all at once. It was more like a switch slowly dimming inside me, quiet, gradual, almost unnoticeable at first. I still loved him. That part of me didn't disappear overnight.

But I didn't trust him anymore. And once that trust cracked, everything else started to fall into place differently.

He came home two days later, apologetic like always.

"I'm sorry," he said softly from the kitchen.

I didn't look up from my laptop.

"You always are," I said, almost automatically.

He sighed, like he was carrying the weight of something heavy but familiar.

"I'm serious this time."

I almost laughed, not because it was funny, but because the words didn't mean anything to me anymore. I had heard them so many times they stopped landing anywhere real inside me.

Still, I nodded.

I didn't have the energy to fight. Life didn't pause just because something inside me had broken open.

I worked. I studied. I took care of my child. I kept moving through the days like I was holding everything together with quiet discipline and habit.

And him… he tried.

For a little while.

But the shift wasn't in him anymore. It was in me.

I stopped reaching. Stopped correcting. Stopped reacting the way I used to when things didn't feel right.

I let him go out. I let him say what he wanted. I let him move how he moved through the world without stepping in, without interrupting, without trying to make sense of it out loud.

No arguments. No explanations. No defending how I felt.

I just watched.

And I think that unsettled him more than anything ever had.

Because I wasn't reacting anymore.

I wasn't chasing answers.

I wasn't trying to fix what kept breaking between us.

I was just there.

Present.

Quiet in a way that said more than anything I could've argued out loud.

But I wasn't invested the same way anymore. And the crazy part was… the more I pulled back, the more he started paying attention.

"Why you so quiet?"

"You good?"

"You acting different."

I would just nod. "Yeah… I'm good." Because explaining it felt pointless.

I wasn't trying to make him understand me. But while he thought I was just being quiet, I was already moving differently, smarter.

I started paying attention to everything. Finances. Schedules. Patterns. What I needed. What my baby needed. What life would look like without him in it.

I didn't say anything. Didn't make threats. Didn't announce my plans. I had learned that every time I spoke too soon, he found a way to manipulate the situation.

So this time, I kept it to myself.

I started saving, little by little. Moving things around. Making sure I had options. Making sure I wasn't stuck. I wasn't trying to fix the relationship anymore. I was preparing to leave it.

And that shift was quiet, but powerful.

I wasn't operating from emotion anymore. I was operating from clarity. And once you see something clearly, you can't unsee it.

I stopped letting my guard down.

At night, I started putting my purse inside my pillowcase, right under my head, my money, my cards, my ID. Everything.

The first night I did it, I felt crazy. Laying there like that, hyperaware of every sound, every movement in the house.

But once he stole from me, I refused to give him another chance.

Some nights, I would wake up out of nowhere.

Just to check if he was still there. On other nights…

I would hear the front door open, then close quietly behind him.

Like he believed I wouldn't notice. But I noticed everything now, the late nights,

the secret calls, the silence that followed him into the house.

The way he would shower as soon as he got home. The distance that lived in him.

The mood swings. The shifting energy I could never predict.

One evening…

I was sitting at the table doing my homework when it hit me.

I had spent years…

trying to save this marriage. Years trying to fix something that was never mine to fix.

Fighting demons…

that didn't belong to me.

And somewhere in all of that… I forgot what peace felt like.

I was always waiting. Waiting for the next problem, the next argument,

the next call.

The next breakdown. The next apology.

It never stopped.

And I was tired. Deeply tired.

But even then…

a part of me still reached for something good. One last good memory to hold onto.

So when his birthday started getting close… I planned a trip.

Something beautiful. Peaceful.

Far away from everything that had been weighing us down, Jamaica.

I invited family. Friends.

Couples we were close to. A full birthday getaway.

And while I was planning it… I let myself believe again.

Maybe this would remind him.

Maybe being surrounded by love would wake something in him again. Maybe he would remember who he was.

Maybe I would get my husband back.

But what I didn't know then… was that this trip…

the one I planned with so much love…

was about to expose the biggest truth of all.

CHAPTER 17

The Message

Jamaica was supposed to be a celebration.

The sun was perfect, too perfect in a way that made everything feel staged for happiness. The ocean breeze drifted through the open space like it was trying to smooth out every rough edge of my thoughts. The villa I rented was everything I had pictured. Big. Open. Sitting right above the water like it belonged there.

A pool sat on the property for everyone to enjoy, exactly what I had imagined when I planned this trip.

Family started arriving, one after the other, their energy filling the space before their bags even hit the floor. They were excited in that loud, effortless way people are when they haven't seen each other in a while. Friends greeted each other like no time had passed at all. Couples unpacked while already talking, plans, drinks, excursions, birthday dinners.

Everything looked normal. Easy.

And he looked happy.

Andre was laughing with his brother, shoulders loose, voice warm. Joking with his best friend like there was nothing behind it, nothing underneath it. He moved through the space like everything in his life had always been this light.

I stood there watching him.

And something settled in my chest that I hadn't felt in a long time.

Pride.

I did this. I planned all of it, every detail, every arrangement, every late-night decision that had stretched over weeks. And seeing everyone together like this… it made it feel worth it.

Later that afternoon, I stepped away.

Just for a moment.

I pulled out my phone.

It was still on airplane mode from the flight. The second I turned it off, everything came rushing in at once, notifications, messages, the noise of my digital life snapping back into place through my social media accounts.

And then one message stood out.

Instagram.

From someone I didn't know.

"Hi. I need to speak with you about your husband."

I frowned, staring at it a little longer than I meant to. Then I opened it.

Another message followed.

"I have pictures, videos, and messages that you need to see."

My stomach tightened.

Not slowly. Not gently.

All at once.

Then another message came through.

"Please send me your email so I can send everything."

And just like that…

the peace I had felt a few minutes earlier was gone. My heart picked up speed, thudding harder in my chest like it had been caught off guard.

My thoughts scattered immediately.

Is this someone trying to start drama? Someone jealous?

Someone just looking for attention?

Or…

something real?

I took a slow breath, trying to steady myself before I moved.

Then I walked over to him. "Hey," I said quietly.

He looked up at me like he already knew what this was about. "What's up?"

I handed him my phone and watched his face closely.

Nothing really changed. No hesitation. No reaction that gave anything away.

"You believe this shit… it's fake," he said quickly.

I blinked. "What do you mean, fake?"

"It's AI," he said, brushing it off like it was obvious. "That person has been trying to blackmail me."

I didn't respond right away.

I knew it was him. Not some AI. Not some random person. Him.

But I swallowed it down.

He must think I'm slow.

"You sure?" I asked anyway, keeping my voice even.

He scoffed. "Wtf, yeah I'm sure. Block them now."

I hesitated.

Because something about it still didn't sit right with me.

But then I looked around.

Everyone was laughing, eating, enjoying themselves. The trip I had planned was finally happening, the atmosphere I had worked so hard to create still holding together.

And the last thing I wanted was to be the reason it fell apart.

So I did what he said.

I sent my email. Blocked the account. Locked my phone.

And told myself it didn't matter, for now.

Because the truth doesn't always come crashing in all at once.

Sometimes… it whispers first.

Just enough to plant something small inside you.

And that message?

It wasn't random.

It was a warning.

And I didn't know it yet…

but that moment was the beginning of everything falling apart.

CHAPTER 18

The Night Everything Broke

The night started beautifully.

The air was warm, heavy with saltwater and something faintly sweet, tropical, clinging to the skin like memory. I had planned a private dinner party on the beach, set right beneath the sunset as if I could somehow freeze it there.

The sky melted into soft layers of orange, pink, and gold, stretching across the ocean like a painting that refused to end. Music played low in the background, soft enough to feel more like a pulse than a sound.

A live drummer kept rhythm on Cuban-style drums, the beat syncing with the waves as if the ocean itself had learned the pattern. A man on stilts moved through the crowd, entertaining, drawing laughter with every exaggerated step. Waiters wove smoothly between guests, serving plates, refilling glasses, carrying out shots of 1942 like it was nothing at all.

Laughter filled the space. Glasses lifted. Conversations overlapped in easy chaos.

Behind us, the villa glowed under soft yellow lights, casting a warm golden wash over everything. For a moment, everything looked exactly how I had imagined it, almost too perfect to be real.

I sat at the end of the table, watching it all unfold. The kind of moment I had been hoping for. Something light. Something whole.

He was already drunk.

But that wasn't new. And I told myself I was okay with it, it was his birthday, after all. He moved from group to group, laughing too loudly, ordering more shots every few minutes like the night owed him something.

Then he came over to me.

His steps were slightly unsteady.

He leaned in close to my ear. "Come dance with me."

I took his hand, and we moved together in the fading light of the sunset.

For a moment, I let myself be in it.

When the music shifted and the dance ended, I tried to step away, back toward my seat, back toward the safety of distance.

But he caught my hand.

Pulled me in again.

Closer this time.

His voice dropped against my ear. "Come take a walk with me," he said quietly.

I looked at him.

His voice was different, no playfulness left in it.

"I don't want to talk about anything tonight," I said calmly. "I just want to enjoy the trip."

"Nothing matters right now."

He stared at me, jaw tight, eyes locked like he was trying to hold himself together.

"I just want to explain myself," he said.

"I don't care right now," I whispered.

Then he turned and walked away. No more words.

I watched him disappear toward the villa, then forced myself to stay in the moment, pretending the air around me hadn't just shifted.

Five minutes later, his brother's wife came over.

Her face was panic before she even spoke.

"Maya," she said, breathless. "Andre is tripping out."

"Huh?" I blinked at her.

"He's drunk… and he's spiraling," she added quickly.

"What happened?"

She hesitated, like saying it out loud would make it worse.

"Andre… kicked the front door in."

I froze.

"What?"

"The door was locked and he said we were trying to kick him out… then he forced it open."

"Why would he do something like that? He has the lock code to get in."

"I know," she said, shaking her head. "But he's really out of it now… saying we're all turning on him because you showed us pictures."

"I didn't show y'all anything," I said immediately.

"I know," she rushed. "But he keeps talking about pictures. I don't even know what he means."

Nothing about this made sense.

And the way she said it… it didn't sound like gossip. It sounded like fear.

As I walked toward the house, I could already hear the noise building, voices, movement, something breaking apart.

A tight panic settled in my chest.

I kept thinking: I cannot afford for this to turn into something bigger. Not here. Not in another country. Not like this.

I just needed it to stop.

When I got closer, I saw it.

The front door, kicked in.

I stepped inside.

Wood splintered around the frame. Holes punched into the wall. Furniture shifted like the room had been dragged through something violent.

And then him.

Lying in the middle of it all. Breathing heavy.

His brother and friend had him pinned to the floor, trying to calm him down.

"Bro, relax," one of them said.

"It's not that serious."

But he wasn't hearing any of it.

"I NEED TO TALK TO MY WIFE!"

I stepped into the room, and the moment my eyes landed on him, something in me tightened.

He looked like the version of him I saw the night he stole from me.

His eyes… empty. Detached.

This is not my husband.

This is something else.

They finally let him up.

He rose and stepped toward me. "Let's talk."

But there was nothing calm about the way he moved. Nothing safe. It felt aggressive, like the air around him had shifted.

My cousin and her husband walked into the villa just as the noise pulled them in.

They took one look at the scene.

"Maya, are you alright?" my cousin asked quickly.

"Yeah, she is… I just want to talk to my wife," Andre answered before I could.

"I'm not talking to you… I'm talking to my cousin."

"Can I just talk to my damn wife?"

My cousin stepped closer, her voice firm. "Yeah, you can…

but we're not leaving her alone with you."

They weren't taking any chances.

"How about you sleep it off and we talk in the morning when you're sober," I said, keeping my voice as steady as I could.

His face twisted instantly.

"What the fck… I'm not drunk. You're fake as fck… showing off in front of these people. You wouldn't be shit without me…"

"Just leave it alone," my cousin cut in.

"Tomorrow you're gonna wake up and apologize like you always do."

But he didn't stop.

He slammed his fist into the wall again, another hole tearing into it.

Everyone was shouting now, telling him to calm down before they called the police.

Then my cousin turned to her husband.

"Just put his ass to sleep… I'm tired of his bullshit." Her voice didn't shake. No hesitation at all.

He moved without saying a word.

He came up behind him and wrapped his arm around his neck. There was a brief struggle, quick, chaotic, then it stopped just as suddenly.

His body went limp.

They laid him carefully on the bed.

For a moment, nobody moved.

We all slowly gathered in the living room, like our bodies were following us a few seconds behind our minds, trying to process what had just happened. The air felt heavier now, different.

His brother was the first to break the silence.

"What made him crash out… we were all having fun?"

His wife shook her head slowly. "We've never seen this side of him."

"He was tripping about some pictures," his best friend added.

Before I could even respond, my cousin cut in.

"This ain't nothing new. He's always drinking… he can't control his emotions. Liquor gives him courage."

Then she started talking about the birthday party I had thrown for him a few years back.

"He got faded… tried to fight people… eventually blacked out."

They carried him out of the club on a stretcher.

He spent the night in the hospital.

The room shifted as she spoke. Their expressions changed, subtle at first, then unmistakable, because they didn't know. None of them did.

I had been holding all of this alone.

But how could they know? They lived far away. They never had to sit with this version of him.

To them, everything always looked fine.

The questions kept coming.

"So why was he so desperate to talk to you tonight… and what pictures was he worried about you showing us?" his sister-in-law asked.

I didn't answer right away.

I just stood there for a moment, breathing through the pressure in my chest.

Then I reached for my phone.

Opened my email.

Scrolled.

Opened the messages.

And handed it over.

Videos.

Pictures.

Screenshots.

Proof.

Him.

With trans women.

One by one, their faces changed.

Shock.

Disbelief.

His brother stared at the screen, his eyes fixed like he couldn't quite process what he was seeing.

"That's not him…"

But even as the words left his mouth, there was something in his face that didn't fully stand behind them.

The truth was right there, staring back at all of us. I felt it settle in the room, heavy and unmistakable. My gaze moved slowly across everyone gathered there, taking in the silence, the tension we were all pretending wasn't spreading between us.

"Don't bring this up at all," I said quietly.

No one argued.

No one even hesitated.

They just nodded, one after another, like the decision had already been made long before I said it out loud.

The next morning…

he woke up smiling. Laughing like nothing had happened. Moving through the day with this ease that felt almost rehearsed. Just like my cousin had said he would.

And everyone played along.

But something in the air had shifted.

It wasn't loud. It wasn't obvious.

It was just there, between the glances, the pauses, the way people spoke a little softer than before, like we were all carefully stepping around something we could no longer unsee.

Because everybody knew now.

Still… we continued with our vacation like nothing had

happened.

CHAPTER 19

The Silence After Jamaica

The flight home from Jamaica was quiet.

Everyone looked drained, like the trip had already been packed away in their minds and replaced with the need to just get home. People sat in their seats pretending everything was normal, but it wasn't.

Conversations stayed short. Eye contact didn't last.

The laughter from earlier in the trip was gone, like it had never existed.

He sat next to me like nothing had happened, scrolling through his phone as if the past few days didn't carry weight.

He made small talk.

Like what happened three nights ago didn't exist at all.

And me…

I couldn't stop staring out the window the entire flight, my reflection faint against the glass, my mind replaying what had been emailed to me over and over again. It wasn't just in my thoughts, it felt lodged there, like it had burned itself into place.

When we got home…

the tension didn't stay behind at the airport. It followed us through the door, into the house, into the silence between us.

He dropped his bags by the entrance.

And just like that, his energy shifted.

"You told them… didn't you?" he said.

I turned slowly.

"Don't start with me."

"I know you showed them those fake videos."

My jaw tightened.

"So, it's fake now?"

He crossed his arms.

"So you think I'm fucking gay?"

I stared at him, letting the question hang in the space between us.

"Hey… it makes sense… you saw the videos."

"I saw edited videos," he snapped. "People can make anything now."

"Well it would explain everything, but I don't care."

That landed heavier than I expected.

"So now you don't care," he said sharply. "You must be fucking someone and trying to project it onto me."

I laughed, short, disbelieving.

That's when his anger rose.

For the next hour, he denied everything. Every video. Every message. Every piece of proof I had. According to him, it was all lies, manufactured by me so I could be with some new guy I'd been sneaking around with. That I was trying to ruin him. To destroy his reputation.

Eventually…

I stopped arguing.

Not because I believed him, but because it felt rehearsed. Like he had already lived this argument in his head too many times, memorized every exit, every accusation, every deflection.

Days passed.

And then…

another message came.

Same person.

This time, everything started to unravel.

She backpedaled on everything she had sent me, denying every word.

"Everything was a lie… I was just mad… I faked those images…"

I stared at the screen and typed back, "How do you know him… why would you make images of him with Trans…"

Minutes later, she replied.

"I met him through mutual friends and we connected, but he told me he had a wife and showed me all your pictures and social media…"

I replied, "Yeah, ok… take care."

I didn't know what to believe anymore, so I stopped

responding. But the night of our wedding kept creeping into my head like it refused to leave.

The next day, she sent a screenshot of a text thread between them.

"He told me to message and say everything I sent was fake… that he would pay me."

My heart started racing.

Another message came through immediately.

"He told me to say I made it all up."

Then another.

"But I'm done playing his games."

I froze as the messages kept coming.

"Our relationship was a transaction."

"He paid me to keep quiet."

"But he stopped paying."

"So now he can deal with the truth."

A cold wave moved through me as I read it.

Then came the proof.

Screenshots. CashApp transactions. Hotel receipts. Messages.

Each one made it harder to dismiss than the last.

Then another message appeared, and everything in me went still.

"I need you to know something else."

"I slept with your husband on multiple occasions… we were

in a relationship… he told me he loved me…"

Another message followed.

"I'm transgender. I still have my original parts."

I just stared at the screen.

At the photos.

At the reality I had been living beside without ever seeing.

Then the final message came through.

"Check his phone."

"Look at his CashApp. Look at his messages. Everything is there."

"Not just with me, but with my friends also."

I slowly lowered my phone.

My heart was beating so loudly it filled my ears.

All the disappearing acts… all the time he spent with his friends… it started to make sense in a way I didn't want it to.

He guarded that phone like it held his entire life.

He kept changing the passcode, always something new, like he didn't trust even his own memory to stay still. At night, when he slept, he powered it off completely, like the phone itself could betray him if it stayed awake without him.

He never let it out of his sight. Not even for a second.

So today, I watched him instead.

Every time his thumb moved across the screen, every time the lock clicked open, I paid attention, quiet, careful, pretending it meant nothing.

So, I could memorize the code without him ever knowing I was learning it.

CHAPTER 20

The Phone

He fell asleep drunk on the couch that night, like nothing in his world had just collapsed.

I sat in the bedroom, heart racing, staring at the door like it might answer me.

The thought wouldn't leave me alone, his phone. I needed the truth, even if it ruined me. So I got up.

I walked into the living room. He was already snoring, completely gone.

His phone was right there on the table, like it had been placed there on purpose… like it had been waiting for me.

My hands started shaking the moment I picked it up. I pressed the screen on. Typed in the code. It unlocked. Just like that.

For the next hour, I disappeared into it.

Texts. Emails. Messages. Photos. CashApp. Snapchat. Everything.

He hadn't deleted anything.

The truth unraveled itself slowly, violently, message after message, payment after payment, conversation after conversation.

Arrangements. Meetups. Explicit details. Constant. Repeated.

It wasn't just one person. There were many

More than six. Different names. Different cities. Different dates stretching across years I thought I understood.

Every time I believed he was just working out with friends… every time I gave him the benefit of the doubt…

he was somewhere else, living a completely different life.

Right next to me.

I don't even know what made me look in his deleted folder… but I did. And it wasn't empty. It never was.

There it was. Their conversation, dated before our trip.

He already knew in Jamaica she was going to message me. He said he was going to call her bluff… and she did. Just like that.

He told her he loved her. That he was only with me for my money. That they were going to run away together.

I stared at the screen.

And it felt like the air just left my body. Like something inside me collapsed without warning.

She was angry because he didn't invite her to Jamaica. Said he was using her. Lying to her. And then she told him to pay her, or she was going to tell me everything.

After that… I don't remember deciding anything.

I just blacked out.

Next thing I knew, I was in the kitchen. Filling a pot with water. My hands didn't feel like mine.

I walked back into the room and threw it straight onto his face.

He shot up instantly.

"What the fuck!"

"Get out of my house!" I screamed.

He just stared at me, confused. Half asleep. Trying to piece reality together.

"What tf happened now?" he said, like I was the problem. "Yo, you're bugging."

I grabbed his phone and threw it at him. It barely missed.

"Your phone!" I yelled. "Your hoe's!"

His eyes snapped open wider.

"You went through my phone?"

"Yeah, I did!"

"N***a, you're gay!"

"You're getting fucked in the ass!" he snapped back. "You nasty dk-ass n*a! Fucking escorts, men, transgender… wtf is wrong with you!"

"What, I don't give you enough p***y? I fuck you every time you want it!"

My voice shook, but not from fear.

From rage.

"All this time…"

"You said you loved me."

"You didn't love me."

My voice cracked on the last word.

"You envied me." He shot to his feet.

"You don't know what you're talking about." But I was done swallowing shit just to keep the peace. "You studied me!" I shouted.

"You studied how I move. How I love. How I live."

Every word tore out of me like it had been waiting for years. "You wanted to be me."

"You wanted to be a fucking bitch."

"All you had to do was ask me to bend you over and fuck you like one."

And just like that, he snapped.

His hand came out of nowhere, sharp, heavy, slapping the words clean out of my mouth.

My body hit the floor before I even registered the pain.

But I didn't stay down.

I got back up.

On some Tina Turner energy, the night she finally fought Ike Turner back in that limo. Something in me had shifted. I wasn't scared anymore.

Not of him.

All I saw in front of me was someone I had lost every ounce of respect for.

I reached into the closet and grabbed the bat. My hands were steady, even if everything inside me wasn't.

"If you don't leave right now…"

"I'm going to beat your head until I see meat."

He just stared at me.

And for the first time… he saw it.

Not fear. Not hesitation. Something else.

He picked up his phone, walked outside, and called the police.

Minutes later, they were there standing between us, escorting him out like I was the threat.

He told them I was crazy. Aggressive.

I stood there with a bruise already rising on my face, my lip split open from his slap. He was drunk.

I told them the truth, that he hit me, and I protected myself.

I told them I didn't want to be the reason another Black man ended up in the system. That I just wanted him gone.

That I had to protect myself.

I had more to lose.

When the door finally closed behind him… something in me broke.

I screamed.

Then I collapsed, my body folding into itself as panic took over. My chest tightened, thoughts racing, what if, what if, what if.

I needed to get tested. Immediately.

My hands were shaking when I called a close friend.

She didn't hesitate. She said she'd come with me.

CHAPTER 21

The Last Call

Days passed.

My test results came back negative.

I was relieved.

I hadn't heard from him, and I didn't care.

I was done.

I kept my focus on what was in front of me, trying to make sense of everything without letting it break me.

Then my phone rang.

His name lit up the screen.

I declined the call.

He called again.

I stared at the screen, my thumb hovering for a moment.

Part of me didn't want to answer.

But I did.

The call connected.

His face filled the screen.

He was sitting on the floor…

in what looked like a hotel hallway.

Crying.

"I miss my family," he said, his voice cracking.

"I'm sorry."

I didn't say anything.

I just looked at him.

I wasn't looking at the man I loved anymore.

I was looking at the man he had chosen to become.

A man fighting demons.

"I'm not gay," he said quickly.

"It was the cocaine."

"The drugs made me do those things."

His voice sounded broken.

Desperate.

But I had heard it all before.

Even now…

he still wasn't taking accountability.

I drew in a slow breath, steadying myself.

And when I finally spoke…

my voice came out sharper than I expected firm, unyielding.

"I can't help you anymore."

He wiped at his face. "Please…"

I shook my head, even though he couldn't see me.

"This is in God's hands now."

And for the first time…

I meant it.

I wasn't trying to fix him.

Wasn't trying to save him.

Wasn't trying to hold on.

I was letting go.

The call ended, and the silence that followed felt heavy, almost unfamiliar.

I just sat there, phone still in my hand, breathing into the quiet.

For the first time in years…

I chose me.

PART V— BREAKING POINT

CHAPTER 22

Won't Let Go

I thought it would be over.

I thought the nightmare had finally ended.

But it didn't.

If anything…

that's when it got worse.

At first, it was the calls.

Back-to-back.

Dozens of them.

Voicemails. Messages.

FaceTime.

"I miss my family."

"Please talk to me."

"I'll change."

I stopped responding.

That's when the anger came.

The apologies disappeared like they had never meant anything.

"You think you can just throw me away?"

"I made you."

"When I see you… you're going to regret this."

Sometimes his voice sounded slurred, like he was drunk. Or high. Or both. I could never tell anymore.

I blocked his number.

But that didn't stop him.

New numbers.

Emails.

Social media messages.

Every notification felt like a warning.

My chest would tighten before I even opened my phone.

Like he was getting closer.

Watching.

Waiting.

Then one evening, my phone rang.

It was my neighbor.

"Hey… Andre's been at your house."

My stomach dropped.

"What do you mean?"

"He's been coming in and out… like he still lives there."

In reality… he did.

He still had a key.

And legally…

he was still my husband.

Which meant…

he didn't see himself as gone.

He saw himself

as someone who still had access.

To everything.

This wasn't over.

Not even close.

CHAPTER 23

Honey, I'm Home

Weeks passed, and he was back home like nothing had happened like he always did.

I told myself to just ignore him. I slept on the couch for days, curling into myself like I could disappear into the cushions if I stayed still long enough. I cooked dinner but never made his plate. I hated that version of me, the one still performing duties in a house that didn't feel like mine anymore. It felt like he had lied to me, broken something inside me, and then just carried on like nothing cracked.

Do you know what it feels like to wait for test results, wondering if your life is about to split in two? I cried while waiting for mine. Not just crying spiraling. Thinking ahead, planning the "what if." What if I was positive. What would my life become then? Who would I have to tell? Who would I lose? My mind kept building futures I didn't ask for, while I sat in the present trying not to fall apart.

He seemed apologetic at first.

He tried to act like he was changing.

But I knew. I knew it was a stunt, something carefully put together just to wheel me back in. And it didn't take long for him to notice that I wasn't responding the way I used to.

My distance.

My silence.

My resistance.

"You been acting funny lately," he said one night, his eyes fixed on me like he was studying a version of me he didn't recognize anymore. I didn't look up.

"I don't think I'm acting funny," I said quietly. "I'm just tired."

"Tired of being the clown in your circus," I added, finally lifting my eyes. He moved closer.

Too close.

"You don't talk to me no more," he said

I shrugged slightly, keeping my voice even. "I talk when there's something to say."

That landed. I saw it in his face, the flicker of discomfort, the shift in control slipping just slightly out of his hands.

I wasn't trying to fix anything between us anymore.

My attitude stayed up whenever he was around. My tone stayed sharp, my words careful but cutting enough to keep distance between us. It made him uncomfortable and I knew it did.

A few days later, he switched.

Completely.

Flowers appeared.

Random compliments followed, slipping into the air like nothing had ever been broken.

"Let me take you out."

"I miss us."

"I know I ain't been perfect, but I'm trying."

Trying.

That word again.

The same one that used to keep me stuck.

I was already exhausted from this emotional rollercoaster… still.

A small part of me wanted to believe it. Wanted to fall back into it, because it was familiar. Because it was easier. Because, in some twisted way, it still felt good.

But I knew better now.

This wasn't change.

This was a pattern. A cycle.

And I had finally reached the point where I was done repeating it.

CHAPTER 24

The Home That Wasn't Safe

One afternoon…

I was at work. Trying to focus.

When my phone rang. It was my friend.

Her voice… panicking.

"Maya… you need to come home." "What's wrong?"

She hesitated. "Your house…" "It's full of people."

"Andre is having a party." Something in my chest sank. I didn't ask another question. I left.

The entire drive home… my mind was racing.

When I pulled up… I already knew.

Cars lined the street. Cars I didn't recognize. Too many of them.

My heart started pounding. I walked to the door…

And the moment it opened…

I smelled nothing but cigarettes and weed smoke. He was letting people smoke inside of my home. My stomach turned.

I stepped inside…

and it looked like chaos. Bottles everywhere.

Music blasting.

People sitting, standing, laughing. Like this was normal.

Strangers.

Faces I had never seen in my life. He was literally having a party. For a second…

I just stood there. Taking it in.

Trying to process how my home… became this.

Then the room went quiet. All eyes on me.

Some of them got nervous. Started grabbing their things. Leaving.

Because they knew.

They weren't supposed to be there. And I was about to crash out.

And then… I saw him.

Sitting on the couch. Relaxed.

Like none of this was a problem.

Like I was the one interrupting something. "This is my house too," he said.

Casual.

Like it didn't matter. Like *I* didn't matter.

My hands started shaking. "You need to get tf out." My voice was low.

Controlled.

But underneath it… was fire.

He laughed. Actually laughed.

"I'm not going no fucking where and neither are they. We're

married."

"This is my house also."

I blacked out.

I didn't give af anymore.

This wasn't just disrespect anymore. This was control.

And if I didn't take it back…

there would be nothing left of me… or my home.

So, I grabbed a beer bottle.

And whacked him across his head with it.

CHAPTER 25

Living With Fear

After that day…

He wasn't just refusing to leave. He was trying to break me.

Piece by piece.

Some nights… I would wake up out of nowhere.

That feeling.

Like someone was watching me.

And one night… I opened my eyes.

And there he was. Standing over the bed, just… staring at me.

My heart stopped.

"What are you doing here?" I whispered.

"I live here," he said.

Calm.

Like nothing about that moment was wrong.

Like standing over me in the dark… was normal.

I sat up, shaken.

"You need to leave my room."

He didn't react.

He just walked out.

Making me fearful of him.

And it didn't stop there.

He started showing up everywhere.

Places I didn't tell him about. My friends' houses.

Parking lots. Work.

Always close enough to remind me he could reach me.

Anytime.

One night…

I walked outside my friend's house.

Glass.

Everywhere.

Shattered across the driveway.

My car…

Destroyed. Windows smashed.

All four tires flattened.

My friend ran out behind me. "Did he do this?"

I didn't answer. Because I already knew. I called the police.

When they arrived…

I told them everything. The threats.

The harassment. The damage.

The officer listened. Then sighed.

And what he said

felt like another betrayal.

"Because you're still married… this is a civil matter."

I stared at him.

"So, he can just destroy my things or worse kill me and there's nothing you can do?"

He shrugged.

"Legally… property between spouses is shared."

Shared.

The word echoed in my head.

"What's yours is technically his."

"And what's his is yours."

Meaning…

he could break anything. Destroy anything.

And there was almost nothing I could do.

This wasn't just emotional anymore.

This wasn't just heartbreak.

This was a fight.

A war.

And he wasn't going to let me walk away peacefully.

CHAPTER 26

No More Living a Lie

For a long time…

I kept everything from my family. Not to protect him.

But to protect them.

I didn't want them to worry. Didn't want them involved. So I dealt with it alone.

I went to God instead.

They knew things weren't perfect.

But they had no idea how bad it really was. Until I made a decision.

If I kept hiding it…

they would never understand the danger I was living in.

So I invited them for the weekend.

Didn't tell him they were coming. I wanted them to see it.

For themselves.

A few days later… they arrived.

My brothers. My sister.

And sister-in-law.

That night, we went out to dinner. And for a few hours…

I forgot about all the chaos that was happening to me. We laughed.

Talked.

Shared stories.

I was able to just relax with them.

But when we pulled back into my driveway… I saw him.

Sitting on the porch. Waiting.

The car went quiet. Everyone saw him. I stepped out.

And immediately… he stood up

Started walking toward me.

But then…

He saw my brothers. And just like that… his energy changed.

He walked right past me. Like I didn't exist.

Reached out his hand.

"Wassup man," he said. "How you been." Casual.

Like nothing had happened.

Like he hadn't been threatening me. Like he hadn't been terrorizing my life.

But as he passed me to greet my brother… he leaned in.

Just enough for me to hear. "You bitch."

I laughed.

But one of my brothers caught it.

I don't know if he heard it… or read his lips.

But the moment Andre reached out his hand

My brother swung. Hard.

Andre dropped instantly. His body hit the ground.

Silence.

Complete silence.

Then my sister-in-law yelled, "Damn you got knocked tf out."

Everyone laughed.

He didn't move.

My sister and my other brother… just stepped over him.

Walked into the house like nothing happened.

"Wait!" I called out.

"Yall not going to help me get him up!"

They turned around.

My sister said, "Not our problem."

They had seen enough.

And in their eyes…

he had crossed the line.

So I was left outside.

Alone.

I knelt beside him, shaking him.

Trying to wake him up.

After a few minutes… he groaned.

Came back. Barely.

I helped him up into the car and drove him to the hospital.

When the doctor asked what happened… he laughed.

Apparently he was intoxicated.

"Her brother knocked me out."

I stepped in quickly.

"What," I said.

"But I asked for it," he said.

The doctor looked at us… confused.

Then left.

When he came back… the truth was clear.

His jaw was broken. He needed surgery. Wires.

I still felt sorry for him I had compassion.

And that's the one thing I didn't life about myself

Someone can do me so dirty and I would still have compassion So I brought him home.

Let him recover.

My family didn't like it. But that's who I was.

I showed grace…

even when it wasn't deserved.

Over the next few days… he proved them right.

Petty. Provoking.

Trying to get a reaction out of them. But they didn't give him one

They ignored him because I asked them to. Until one morning.

I opened the blinds.

Let the sunlight in.

Trying to start the day fresh. Turned on some music

And started to cook breakfast for everyone Suddenly

He grabbed the curtains. Yanked them shut.

I goes back to open them. He pushed my hand away.

My sister-in-law saw everything. And before anyone could react She ranned up on him.

Fast.

Yelling, "You hit my sister." Punch after punch landed. Everyone rushed in.

Pulled her back.

Before it escalated any farther. Everyone asks "what happened."

"I saw him put his hand on her" she said He grabbed his phone.

"I'm calling the police!"

I looked at him.

"It's your word against ours."

"And you're already known for chaos." He stormed outside.

Waited on the porch for the police to arrive Like a damn snitch While he sat there…

My sister quietly changed the locks.

I meant to change them weeks ago but never had the time By the time the police arrived

It was already done. He told his story.

"She changed the locks and had her sister attack me!" The officers turned to me.

"What's going on?"

"We're getting a divorce," I said. "He should not be here."

They barely acknowledged it.

Then one of them said something… "You still have to give him a key."

I blinked. "What?"

"You're still legally married."

"If he lives here, you can't lock him out. If you don't give him a key… we can take you to jail."

I felt the anger rise.

But I stayed calm.

I handed him a key.

They told him to leave until everyone calmed down. And once they were gone…

We changed the locks again.

This time… I wasn't alone.

My family finally saw everything that I was hiding. Within days my family saw that I was living in hell.

The next time I would see him… would be…

in a courtroom.

PART VII — WAR AFTER LEAVING

CHAPTER 27

Divorce court

Divorce court…

wasn't the freedom I thought it would be. It felt like another battlefield.

The first day I walked in… he was already there.

Looking all innocent. But he wasn't alone. Sitting next to him… was another woman.

Well, she looked like a woman. I couldn't tell.

With his track record.

I had never seen her before. They sat close.

Whispering. Comfortable. Like a couple.

This is why I haven't seen him… someone else has occupied his time.

The woman sitting beside him…

was the one he had been staying with. There for "support."

I didn't react. At that point…

nothing about him surprised me anymore.

When the judge started reviewing everything… I listened.

Everything I had lived through.

And then the decision came. Joint custody.

Week on. Week off.

My heart dropped. After everything… The threats.

The harassment. The police.

The restraining order.

None of it mattered enough.

The court still believed…

my child needed both parents. I didn't have a choice.

But I realized this is good for me.

I can work and focus more on school since I was almost done. I can start putting my life together.

Before every visit…

Divorce court…

wasn't the freedom I thought it would be. It felt like another battlefield.

The first day I walked in… he was already there.

Looking all innocent. But he wasn't alone. Sitting next to him… was another woman.

Well, she looked like a woman. I couldn't tell.

With his track record.

I had never seen her before. They sat close.

Whispering. Comfortable. Like a couple.

This is why I haven't seen him… someone else has occupied his time.

The woman sitting beside him…

was the one he had been staying with. There for "support."

I didn't react. At that point…

nothing about him surprised me anymore.

When the judge started reviewing everything… I listened.

Everything I had lived through.

And then the decision came. Joint custody.

Week on. Week off.

My heart dropped. After everything… The threats.

The harassment. The police.

The restraining order.

None of it mattered enough.

The court still believed…

my child needed both parents. I didn't have a choice.

But I realized this is good for me.

I can work and focus more on school since I was almost done. I can start putting my life together.

Before every visit…

So that anyone didn't have to worry themselves with it, and to keep their hands out of my child's hair.

Her hair had always been natural. Healthy.

Untouched by heat.

That was important to me. The braids weren't just a style. They were protection.

My way of making sure…

no one could damage her hair. But every time they came

back… her braids…

gone.

Hair messy. Unkept.

Like no one cared.

I tried to ignore it at first.

Told myself maybe it was nothing. Until one day…

She came home with her hair half straightened. I checked her hair.

It was just shedding everywhere. Her hair…

damaged. Dry.

Brittle.

Like someone had taken heat to it and burned it.

I was pissed.

I had never put heat in my child's hair.

I felt like they was doing this on purpose to get a reaction out of me.

So I pushed my emotion to the back. Shampooed and deep conditioned her hair, greased her scalp, and put more braids in. This time small knotless braids.

Because who in their right mind would take down fresh knotless braids? But come the following week…

I was proven wrong.

Her braids was out of her hair. They pulled up to the meeting spot.

He gets out to open the door for our child.

And that's when I saw her hair just wild and untamed.

"Where tf are her braids?" I yelled. "Why is she looking like this?"

"Don't start this shit… my girl felt like they were too tight.. so I let her take them out." I put our child in the car with my sister.

She came with me at every exchange.

"Andre I know your fucking lying…. I don't even braid my child hair tight… I just braided her hair last week… why is that every time I send her there with braids she comes back looking like a dirty ass unkept child."

"You tripping."

"No ni**a you are."

I looked towards the passenger side of the window. There she was.

Ugly.

Dirty looking.

The kind no matter how clean your clothes are, or how much you try to put yourself together and look fresh…

No matter what you do…

You would still have that dirty look to you. Well that was her.

She was grinning out the window towards me.

Like she was doing this on purpose, wanted a reaction from me.

My child was her pawn.

"Don't touch my baby hair again," I said. "Dirty ass bitch."
"ANDRE I"LL SEE YOUR GAY ASS IN COURT."

I turned back towards her.

"I hope you know the ni**a you're fucking and sucking is doing the same thing to men…. But hey you look like one so I get it."

"Why do you have to do this." Andre said.

"Fuck you Andre with a hard stiff one."

"Okay Maya…have a good night."

He got in his; well not his but her car, and they drove off.

I took pictures of my child's hair for documentation.

I was going to show the judge everything. My child was being mistreated.

Something I thought he would never let someone do to her. I felt she was safe being with her father.

Because he loved her.

He was stupid and naive.

I was just getting to adjust and enjoy my weeks to myself.

But I was willing to sacrifice them to be a full-time single mother just to protect my child.

CHAPTER 28

The Court System

The custody exchanges were supposed to happen in front of the courthouse every Tuesday evening.

Neutral ground. Safe.

At least… that's what they called it.

The first time we were supposed to meet there… he never showed up.

I waited. And waited.

Watching the clock. Watching the street. Nothing.

No call.

No message. Just silence.

It was Christmas Eve and I was going to a concert.

This would be my first Christmas without my child since I gave birth to her. My sister was with me.

She was getting impatient.

She got out the car to get some fresh air.

I called the judge phone to leave a message.

"Good evening Judge Starling, this is Maya Brooks. I'm here waiting in the parking lot in front of the courthouse building. I've been here for forty-five minutes waiting for Andre. He is a no show…"

I then called the non-emergency line to see what I should do. Before I can get someone on the line,

my sister asked,

"Is that Andre… it looks like Andre."

Across the street was a car pulled over by police cars. Guns pointed, instructing him to walk backwards.

We walk a little closer. It's him.

I take a picture and a video for documentation. Gets in my car and leave.

No concert for me tonight.

I will be spending Christmas with my child.

"Look at God, want he do it." I said. "Thank you Jesus."

"Amen" my sister replied.

Later his mom calls me… "Andre is in jail."

"Thank you for letting me know… Merry Christmas." I kept it short and simple.

Even though I love her, she was still his mother.

And a mother would do anything to protect their child.

Once I hung up the phone,

I grabbed my computer to check the inmate website. There it was.

Andre Brooks. He was arrested.

Misdemeanor charges: drunk driving.

Ran a red traffic light.

Driving on suspended license.

Two days later… things got worse.

His girlfriend called the judge and told them…

I had reported them.

That I was the one that called the police. Wow.

I just stared when I heard it.

How?

How would I even know where they were? What direction were they coming from?

What kind of car were they driving?

Or if he was the one driving. But somehow…

that lie made its way back to the judge. And just like that…

I became the problem. The narrative shifted.

Now it looked like I was bitter. Angry.

Trying to get back at him. Even though I brought proof. Police reports.

Documentation. But it didn't matter.

Because once the story was flipped… it stuck.

The court believed I was interfering. Interfering with his relationship with our child. Months would pass for the next court date.

I felt like I was living in hell while waiting. I had all of this evidence

To prove neglect and harassment. Photos of them showing up

where I was.

Watching me. Following me.

Evidence of everything I had been living through. Even when I called for a wellness check.

Because my child secretly called me to tell me something that had my blood boiling. She sounded scared.

She said his girlfriend… had gone into a rage.

And tried to stab him.

I wasn't trying to cause problems. I was trying to protect her.

That's it.

But even that…

was turned against me.

Now I was the one "jeopardizing" his parenting time.

And for a while… no one listened.

No one believed me.

And that…

was the hardest part. Standing there… telling the truth…

and watching it get ignored.

By a judge who is supposed to make the best decision for the child.

CHAPTER 29

Finally The Truth

Eventually…

the truth came out. It always does.

Not when you want it to.

Not when you're begging to be heard. But when it's ready.

One day…

he got arrested. For the 3rd time. But this time… Domestic violence. Drug possession.

And the same woman…

the one sitting next to him in court… was the one who called the police.

The same woman he brought for "support."

The same woman who helped twist the story against me. Now…

she was the one telling her truth.

And when it happened…

everything started falling apart for him once again. She began posting.

On his social media. Pictures.

Videos. Messages.

Things I had been trying to explain for months. Things

nobody wanted to believe.

Now…

they could see it. She told everyone.

That he had been meeting men.

That she caught him… in her own home… with another man.

And then she wrote

"I should have believed everything his wife told me." Wife.

Not ex.

Not "baby mama."

Wife.

The truth I carried alone… was no longer mine to prove. It was visible.

Public. Undeniable.

He bailed himself out.

Called my phone on multiple occasions. Of course I didn't answer.

He didn't show up for custody exchanges. Didn't help with our child.

He just went ghost.

When it came time for court… he didn't show up.

The judge felt stupid.

She was always on his side.

Like he had her wrapped around his finger. She believed everything.

And she felt compassion for him.

A black man who just want a chance in life to raise his child.
And here is the bitter black baby momma stopping him.

A bench warrant was issued for his arrest.

The judge read out all of his arrest and conviction.

And this time…

She saw him for who he really was. Not the story he created.

The truth.

She finally believed me. I was granted

Full custody. No visitation.

Eventually…

he turned himself in. One year in jail.

Just like that… everything changed. I sat there… processing it
all.

For so long…

I had been fighting to be heard. Fighting to be believed.

Fighting to protect my child.

I didn't have to fight anymore.

For the first time in months… I could breathe.

PART VII – HEALING & REBIRTH

CHAPTER 30

Jail Call

Several months later… I got a call.

His mother. Three-way line. It was him.

From the jail. His voice… was different. Calmer.

Clear.

Like the Andre I fell in love with.

"I'm sober now," he said.

Sounding like a scene from the movie Color Purple. I didn't respond right away.

Because I had heard versions of this before. But something about this time…

felt different.

He apologized. For everything.

For all the pain he caused me. The pain he caused our family. And then…

He told me about her.

The ex-girlfriend.

He said she was jealous of our child. Didn't like when she came over.

Because she would get so if his attention. Asked him why she was always sitting on his lap.

That it was weird and made her feel weird about it. That no man should have a little girl sitting on their lap. He also said she would mistreat our child.

Do things on purpose… to upset her.

When he wasn't there.

But he didn't know what to believe.

I was pissed just hearing him explain everything.

I wanted to jump through that phone and slap the words out of his mouth.

My thing was he knew. He knew the whole time. But he ignored it.

Because he was high.

Because he needed somewhere to live. A vehicle to drive.

I used that woman.

And my child suffered the consequences.

Because he didn't want to deal with his own problems.

And then he said something… that hit even deeper.

"Part of me wanted you to hurt." Silence.

Because that was the truth. The intention.

He wanted me to feel what he felt.

And hearing that… hurt.

But it didn't break me. Not anymore.

Because by then…

I understood something.

His truth…

was no longer mine to carry.

His pain…

was not mine to fix.

His choices…

were not mine to answer for. And for the first time…

I wasn't trying to understand him. I was finally understanding myself.

"Well you didn't just hurt me," I said, "you hurt our child as well."

"She suffered because of your actions… and I hope and pray you get all the help and answers for yourself while you're in there."

Then I ended the call.

I really wanted to say I hope you rot in jail and don't drop the soap, bitch. But I had to control my emotions.

Don't give him the power I once had before to control them. Because if he controlled my emotions, he still had control over me.

And that's something I would never in my living breath give him again.

I own my power.

CHAPTER 31

The Woman I Became

After everything I survived…

I realized something.

My pain didn't start with him. It started

in my childhood. The yelling.

The beatings.

The constant feeling of being blamed… for things that were never my fault.

I was just a little girl…

trying to survive in a world that didn't feel safe. And I grew up too fast.

For years…

I lived in survival mode. Trying to fix broken people. Trying to earn love.

Trying to prove my worth. But after the divorce…

I made a decision. I was going to heal.

Not just from that marriage. From everything.

I started therapy.

I unpacked it all. The pain I carried.

The patterns I repeated. The little girl inside me… still begging to be seen. Still begging to be loved. And slowly…

I began to understand her. Not judge her.

Not silence her. But heal her.

Therapy changed me. It helped me rebuild… from the inside out.

I learned forgiveness too.

Not because they deserved it. But because I deserved peace.

Holding on to anger… kept me tied to the past.

Letting go… set me free.

I started rebuilding my mind.

Every morning

I spoke life over myself. Affirmations.

Prayer.

Intentional thoughts. Exercising more.

I even joined a running club. I started writing daily…

I couldn't find a journal the would help with my healing, so I decided to build one.

I customized it around how I visualize my healing journey. I named it "90 Days Healing Journal."

Page by page…

I rewired how I saw love. how I saw myself.

I made daily healing goals and process.

I also added

Daily accomplishments

Just to make myself recognize I was achieving my goals. And

then…

something beautiful happened.

I stopped looking for validation. And started giving it to myself.

As time passed…

my life began to change. I finally finished school.

Walked across that stage… with my family in the crowd cheering me on,

proud of me

after everything I had been through. That moment wasn't just about a degree. It was proof.

That nothing I went through… broke me.

It built me.

Made me stronger, wiser

smarter

A few months after my commencement… I opened my own medical spa.

Not just a business. A vision.

A place where beauty met healing. Where confidence was restored.

Where women could walk in one way… and leave feeling like themselves again.

I designed it with intention.

Soft beige. Warm whites. Rich browns.

Hints of gold woven throughout.

Greenery placed perfectly.

Plants bringing life into every corner.

It felt calm.

Elevated.

Peaceful.

Like a reset the moment you walked in.

The waiting area was beautiful.

Clean. Inviting.

With soft seating and natural textures that made you want to sit… and stay.

Everything flowed.

Every detail mattered.

Beyond that…

I created separate suites for every beauty need. Spaces dedicated to the medical side of beauty and the cosmetology side.

Hair. Skin. Nails.

All in one place.

A true one-stop beauty and wellness experience.

Right at the entrance…

I added a small boutique. Surrounded by glass walls.

So clients could see in as soon as they walked through the door.

Products.

Pieces.

A curated extension of the brand.

I built a team.

Women who believed in the vision. Who showed up with passion.

Who wanted more for themselves.

And together…

We created something I once only dreamed about… and finally brought to life.

CHAPTER 32

Reflection

The day of my grand opening… Everything felt different.

Like every step I took to get here… was leading to this exact moment.

The doors opened.

And people came to support. It was packed with people.

Women who had been watching me build from the ground up. Women who saw themselves in me.

The space filled quickly. Laughter.

Conversations.

Compliments flowing from every corner.

"This is beautiful."

"You did this?"

"I'm so proud of you." I smiled.

This was proof.

Proof that I made it through. That I didn't break.

My team moved with purpose. Welcoming clients.

Offering services. Explaining treatments.

Everything flowing exactly how I envisioned it.

The boutique at the front caught everyone's attention. Glass walls reflecting the soft gold accents…

The greenery bringing life into the space.

People stopping.

Looking.

Buying.

Supporting.

I was standing in something I created. Something that was mine.

I looked around slowly. Taking it all in.

Every detail. Every decision.

Every piece of this place… came from a version of me… who refused to give up.

My mind went back.

Back to the woman I used to be. The one who questioned herself. who stayed too long.

who kept trying to fix something… That was breaking her.

The one who thought love meant holding on… No matter how much it hurt.

And then I looked at who I am now. Standing here.

In my own space. my own peace. my own power.

I didn't lose anything. I found myself.

The version of me that was always there… Just buried under pain.

Under doubt.

Under someone else's chaos.

And now?

She was free. Not just from him.

But from everything that made her feel small.

I let out a slow breath of relief.

I didn't feel like I was rebuilding. I felt like I had arrived.

CHAPTER 33

New Maya

Later that night

While home alone, I looked around.

Every part of my home carried a pain.

I needed to fully let go.

There was a decision I needed to make. I decided to sell my home.

That house held too many memories. Too many versions of me…

That I had outgrown.

Too many moments I had tried to forget… but never fully let go of.

It wasn't just a place. It was a chapter.

And I was ready to close it. Fully.

No attachments.

That held so much pain. And I bought a new one. A fresh start.

A peaceful space.

A home filled with laughter… instead of fear.

But the biggest change… was me.

I was a new woman. For most of my life… I wore my hair

short. A pixie cut.

People thought it was just my style. But it wasn't.

Having long hair became something that could be used against me. Something that gave people control.

It was easy to grab me by.

So, when I grew up... I cut it. Short.

My way of protecting myself.

But one day...

I stopped cutting it. Month by month... it grew.

Now it rests on my shoulders. No pain attached to it.

Just... freedom.

My hair grew...

the same way I did. Through patience. Through healing.

Through time.

When people see me now, they see me glowing, happy and free.

They think I found someone new, that I'm in love again.

I smile. Because I did.

Someone strong. loyal.

who would never betray me.

I found myself.

And I love that woman...

more than I ever thought possible.

After everything life tried to take from me... I finally

understood.

The greatest love story of my life… was the one I built with me.

So, if you're reading this…

And you feel like you're losing yourself trying to hold on to someone else, let them go.

And choose you.

EPILOGUE

Choose You

Healing didn't happen overnight.

It didn't manifest in a single, grand moment.

Instead, it manifested through quiet decisions, through establishing boundaries that I once hesitated to set, and through choosing peace, even when it felt unfamiliar.

For a long time, I thought love meant holding on, fighting harder, understanding more, and being patient enough for the both of us.

But I learned the hard way…

Love should never cost you yourself.

Some people enter your life not to journey alongside you, but rather to teach you lessons on what you should no longer tolerate.

And sometimes…

no matter how much you love someone,

no matter how much you see the good in them…

you are not meant to fix them.

You cannot heal someone who refuses to see their own wounds.

You cannot save someone who is comfortable in their chaos.

That is not your assignment.

I wanted to go back sometimes.

To help.

To explain.

To give one more chance.

But I had to learn something that changed everything:

You can't save everyone.

Some people gotta deal with their own karma.

Their own consequences.

Their own lessons… without you getting in the way.

Cause sometimes, what feels like love…

is actually just attachment, trauma, or wanting to be needed.

And when you finally step back…

when you finally choose yourself…

You realize how much energy you wasted trying to fill someone who chose to be empty.

Watch for the signs.

The inconsistency.

The manipulation.

The way they make you doubt yourself.

The way you feel smaller… instead of safe.

Those aren't small things.

They're warnings.

Red flags don't turn green.

They just get harder to ignore.

And honestly...

the longer you stick around, the more you lose parts of yourself.

I had to learn that choosing me wasn't selfish.

It was necessary.

It was survival.

It was healing.

It was growth.

And once I did… everything changed.

My peace got louder than my pain.

My standards got stronger than my loneliness.

My self-love got deeper than any love I'd ever given away.

So, if you're reading this…

If you feel tired…

confused…

or like you've been pouring into someone who keeps taking from you…

This is your sign.

Choose yourself.

Trust what you feel.

Walk away from what breaks you… even if you love it.

Because the life waiting for you on the other side of letting go…

is the one where you finally become

the version of yourself you were always meant to be.

And I promise you…

She's worth it.

AUTHOR BIO

Melissa Bertrand is a licensed cosmetologist, entrepreneur, and healthcare professional with a passion for healing, beauty, and transformation.

Through her journey of overcoming trauma, betrayal, and adversity, she now uses her voice to empower women to reclaim their power, rebuild their confidence, and choose themselves unapologetically.

www.ingramcontent.com/pod-product-compliance
Lightning Source LLC
Chambersburg PA
CBHW061423160726
47995CB00003B/725